Inland
PASSAGES

MAKING A LOWCOUNTRY LIFE

WILLIAM BALDWIN

Published by The History Press
Charleston, SC 29403
www.historypress.net

Cover design by Natasha Momberger.

Back cover image: William "Billy" Baldwin with a Spot-tail Bass of Cape Romain.
Photo by Ben Graham.

First published 2004
Second printing 2008

Manufactured in the United States

ISBN 978-1-59629-034-1

Library of Congress CIP data applied for.

Dedicated to Candy

Other Books By or With William Baldwin

Carolina Plantations
Charleston
Charleston: My Picture Guide to a Holy City
The Fennel Family Papers: A Novel
A Gentleman in Charleston and the Manner of His Death
Gracious Beaufort
The Hard to Catch Mercy
Heaven is a Beautiful Place:
A Memoir of the South Carolina Coast
Journey of a Hope Merchant:
From Apartheid to the Elite World of Solo Yacht Racing
Lowcountry Daytrips:
Plantations, Gardens and a Natural History of the Charleston Region
Lowcountry Plantations Today
Mantelpieces of the Old South:
Lost Architecture and Southern Culture
Mrs. Whaley and Her Charleston Garden
Mrs. Whaley Entertains
The Nature of Beauty
Ornamental Ironwork of Charleston
Plantations of the Low Country
Sacred Places of the Lowcountry
William McCullough, Southern Painter,
in Conversation with William Baldwin, Southern Writer

Contents

Acknowledgements

Many of these interviews and essays appeared previously in other publications. I would like to thank the editors with whom I worked, including Linda Renshaw, Tom Flemming, Steve Hoffius, Pete Rering, Katherine Walton, N. Jane Iseley, Ellen Dugan, Alex Moore and Selden Hill.

Also, I want to thank Jason Chasteen and the staff at The History Press, for their energetic work on this collection.

Preface

Inland Passages strikes me as a perfect title, for this collection deals with passages in almost every sense of the word. The working title was *The Land Comes First.* Looking back over this collection, I realize the title could just as easily have read *The Family Comes First.* Landscape designer Robert Marvin would have approved, for though he insisted "the land comes first," the walls of his and his wife's bedroom were covered with hundreds of family pictures, proof enough that in the Carolina Lowcountry land and family are often synonymous. But, according to Scarlet O'Hara, that is true of the entire South, and I suspect it's true of the entire world—at least the world's rural portions. Land has certainly been a concern of my family. My father, William P. Baldwin Jr., came south as a Fish and Wildlife Service biologist and went on to become a wildlife management consultant and plantation broker. My mother, Agnes Leland Baldwin, was a historian and land title researcher. On salt marsh titles she was probably the best in the business.

Land. I grew up around the topic. I grew up on it, as well. I still am—even at sixty. Still growing up. Still on the land. But I won't try to pass myself off as an environmentalist. I'm more interested in the people and the "story" of the comic, tragic business of history that goes trampling across the Lowcountry's surface. Nevertheless, I see the natural world as a place of intense beauty, even of sacredness. I greatly admire the preservation work of the Nature Conservancy and like-minded organizations and individuals. I hope that comes through.

Many of these interviews and essays were done between 1985 and 1989. I was attempting a book about how, over the centuries, people had used the resources of the Cape Romain marshes that bordered my home in McClellanville, South Carolina. That book never got finished—but chapters appeared in several magazines. Also included are previously published essays and interviews of broader interest, including two interviews taken from oral histories, several unpublished interviews and a pair of speeches that seemed to fit in.

There's a rough order to the collection, a progression of sorts, but feel free to jump around. In short notes—some at the beginning and some at the end—I give my current thoughts on what's presented. I hope what follows brings you pleasure.

A Gift from the Sea

Originally this was to be part of the South Carolina's middle school ecology curriculum and would be used to show how people had interacted with the Sea Island environment and how they'd used their resources. I don't think that project was ever completed but the essay has been taught in the classroom.

The pieces that follow are a bit more personal.

A HOWLING WIND WHIPS THE palmettos, tattering their fronds in its frenzy. Deep-gray waves, capped with white, pile ashore. For days the storm pounds the island, eating away at the beach, threatening its expanse—what humans view as "damage." But such a storm can also be constructive, part of a building process, for it leaves behind sand that will end up in the dunes and even higher ground of the Sea Island.

The term "Sea Island," like "Lowcountry," is not so much a geological description as a cultural one. Beginning at Georgetown and running south into Florida, a thin chain of barrier islands front the Atlantic Ocean. Between them and the mainland are usually wide expanses of salt marsh, bays and twisting tidal creeks. Depending on the definition we use, the Sea Islands are a part of this chain or protected by them or a bit of both. Sullivan's Island, Hilton Head Island and Pinckney Island all have behind them a rich and varied history of uses. To understand how and what these were, though, we must look at the physical makeup of the islands.

Two kinds of islands are involved. Those north of Charleston are generally considered beach ridges. These are ridges of dunes formed by sand thrown up by currents and storms; sand that is then held in place by hearty vegetation. The islands south of Charleston are usually more substantial "erosion remnants," cut off from the mainland by water draining from inland. Generally thicker with their shape being dictated by the meandering of these rivers and creeks, their soil is richer, and compared to the more exposed beach islands they are relatively stable. But at one time these remnant islands were beach ridge islands themselves, perhaps twenty to thirty thousand years ago, and a close look at aerial photographs shows their weathered ridges and valley lines. Also, of course, these remnant islands are fronted or "ghosted" by the dunes where they touch the ocean and are subject to the same "beach ridge" forces.

These forces are strong, for as the moon circles the earth, the earth spins, and tides and currents are set in motion. The Gulf Stream pushes north about seventy miles offshore. It brings warm Caribbean waters that give the Sea Islands a semi-tropical climate. Inshore a south-moving littoral current sweeps down the coast, eroding the northern ends of the islands and building up their southern ends.

Of course, other factors are also at work. Rivers dump silt from vast inland watersheds. Man-made jetties alter the terrain. Prevailing strong winds build up beaches; hurricanes tear them down. And because the earth is warming and the polar ice caps are melting, the sea level is rising. Ten thousand years ago our shoreline extended roughly fifty miles farther to the east. But there have been many such advances—and retreats. The land itself may have tilted. In short, these islands give geologists much to disagree over, so we will clarify matters by simply calling them a gift from the sea.

Along the dune edge, the familiar sea oats catch hold of the sand. Law protects them now, but it's the inland vegetation of these islands that is actually quite unique. Bulls Island is the northernmost reach of what's called the Florida maritime forest, a rich evergreen mixture of live oaks, cedars, wax myrtles, palmettos, smilax, pines and more. The warming influence of the Gulf Stream makes possible this lushness.

Deer, squirrels, alligators, raccoons and a vast array of bird life enjoy this wilderness. The Sea Islands were considered hunting islands by the Indians who summered on the mainland or at least well inland from the ocean. The White settlers did the same, and we see the name preserved in Hunting Island State Park. But early maps also show the Isle of Palms, Dewees Island and Capers Island as "Hunting Islands."

Also important to the Indians was the easily available seafood—evidenced by the oyster, clam, conch and periwinkle shells they left behind in their piles of refuse or middens. Until the advent of carbon dating the Sea Islands were thought to be a cultural backwater, but we now know that pottery was first introduced to North America here. Distinctive fiber tempering and large rings of discarded shells have been dated back nearly forty-five hundred years and suggest at least some sort of contact with the earlier pottery makers of South America. Though these early people had long since disappeared, the tribes greeting the English settlers in 1670 depended on the Sea Island resources in much the same way. And there was immediate conflict.

A look at the map tells the tale. Most of the islands lost their original names when the new arrivals chose to commemorate themselves: Bull, Fripp, Parris and Seabrook. And even the Indian names can be deceptive. The Kiawah tribe was pushed back south to Kiawah Island. The Edisto had been pushed north to Edisto Island. Still, many of the names persist: Stono, Wadmalaw and Ashepoo—at least in abbreviated form—literally hundreds on today's maps. But by the 1730s the Indians themselves had vanished from record. Warfare, slave trading and epidemics had taken their toll.

Settlers raising cattle on the Sea Islands around Beaufort is given as a main reason for the bloody Yemassee Indian uprising of 1714. The Yemassee and their Spanish allies eventually lost. Contrary to popular telling, Daufuskie is probably not "the first key" mispronounced. It's an Indian word, and one of the final battles was fought on that island's Bloody Point in 1728.

The Spanish had come to the Sea Islands two centuries earlier. They often named land for the Catholic Saint's Day on which it was discovered. Santa Elena became St. Helena Island. San Romanas became Cape Romain. And Lady's Island may have been Our Lady originally. The French Huguenots came next and left the name Port Royal. The Scottish dissenters followed. Parris Island was once Scot Island. It's a surprisingly diverse group and a legacy of names that probably depends most on the conservative oral tradition of the early watermen and settlers.

Water provided transportation in those earliest days. While we tend to think of the islands as cut off, they were actually more accessible than much of the mainland. An "inland passage" led behind the islands north of Charleston to the Santee Delta, and another went south to connect with the Savannah River, so it was not necessary to go to sea. At first travelers went by canoe, then by flats and schooners. Well into this century, paddle-wheel steamboats visited the Sea Islands.

Despite threats by the Indians, the Spanish and pirates, the Sea Islands were quickly settled, even before a use for them had been found. Agricultural experiments followed, but none were particularly successful. Cattle thrived, though. They needed no fences and foraged for food. In fact, cattle and sheep weren't removed from some of these islands until fairly recently.

A deforested Old World looked to the New for timbers to build ships and the tar to caulk them. Following the American Revolution, a second harvest of this nature would come. Crews of New England "Live Oakers" moved through, cutting out oak ribs for the ships of our new navy, like *Old Ironsides*.

Burning shell for mortar lime (most of it midden shell) became another enterprise, and later shell would be used for fertilizer.

The first true "plantation" crop, however, was indigo, a plant used in the manufacturing of dye. England offered a bounty for this, and wealth came to the settlers, bringing a plantation system with slave labor, a single cash crop and large land holdings. When the American Revolution brought an end to indigo profits, Sea Island cotton quickly replaced the plant. And the cotton crop, most often associated with the Sea Islands, gives them what we refer to as a cultural identity.

First introduced from the West Indies into Georgia, long staple or Sea Island cotton was planted successfully by William Elliot on Hilton Head Island in 1790. Its fiber was long, strong and fine, producing an expansive cloth that was compared to silk and often brought far higher prices than inland or short staple cotton. It could only be grown along the coast, for it required the semi-tropical temperatures provided by the Gulf Stream.

The islands north of Charleston and along the mainland could grow a slightly inferior "Santee" or "Mains" cotton, but the true success was in the Beaufort area. There, Sea Island property values skyrocketed, and often every available foot was put under cultivation. Seeds were carefully selected and picked cotton was carefully cleaned. Even the sandiest field could produce if fertilized with mud and decayed marsh grass, and this natural fertilizer surrounded the islands. The disadvantage, however, was that this work was done by hand. Inventories often show hundreds of hoes and not a single plow. The slave population increased, the White population isolated themselves from the growing censure of the world. Edisto Island threatened to secede from the Union on her own, a sentiment shared through many of the islands.

Planters built their mansions, educated their sons abroad and even married their daughters to European aristocracy. But only eighty years after the establishment of the cotton plantations, the Civil War began. Robert E. Lee was placed in charge of coastal defenses. He visited the Sea Islands and declared them indefensible—which they were. Early in the war the Union navy entered Port Royal and, after a brief encounter with island batteries, captured Beaufort. Most of the surrounding Sea Islands were abandoned to the enemy.

The Sea Islands' antebellum "Golden Age" had ended and a new order began. The Port Royal experiment gave freed slaves property of their own, and when General Sherman passed by at the end of the war he did the same. However, much confusion surrounded this redistribution. Though encumbered by legal cases that dragged on for years, some original owners did manage to return. Cotton planting resumed, but only with limited success.

Low-lying areas had always been vulnerable to hurricanes. The storm of 1893, however, was particularly damaging in lives lost and land taken out of cultivation. By 1920 the boll weevil halted cotton planting for good. But the planters had always been able to raise staple crops, and "truck farming" came to the islands next. Potatoes, tomatoes, corn and cucumbers are still being grown commercially in a few places. Phosphate was mined for fertilizer on Johns Island and in the Beaufort area, but heavy taxing during the 1890s ended that. By the beginning of the century, however, timber companies were purchasing acreage, and Yankee sportsmen interested in quail and duck hunting had also begun to buy up the old plantations.

Oyster canneries still provided income for the descendants of the freed slaves. The men picked the banks using small bateaus, and their wives shucked. Small gardens and fishing supplemented these earnings. But opportunities for the Black population were dwindling. The migration north spread as the Great Depression brought additional hardships. So, at a time when roads were being paved and bridges were finally beginning to replace steamboats, the population of the Sea Islands was actually shrinking.

The overwhelming majority of this population was Black. With Blacks outnumbering Whites ten-to-one and even a hundred-to-one, it's not surprising that an isolated and unique Black culture would have survived. Even before the 1860s, this culture was firmly entrenched in the slave streets or communities, and freedom, in part, meant the freedom to preserve African traditions. Using a vocabulary of mostly English words and African sentence structure, the slaves developed a Creole language called Gullah—a dialect their White owners would often come to speak and which is still occasionally heard today. Along with this language, the Black Sea Island communities also preserved their spirituals, woodcarving and storytelling—all of it richly textured by their African heritage. Churches were usually the center for these communities, but in the years following the Civil War, benevolent societies and militias also offered aid and preserved community values. On St. Helena Island, the Penn Center, begun as part of the Port Royal experiment, was instrumental in maintaining the old ways and preserving the new.

Times change, however, and it is more difficult to find evidence of either antebellum plantation culture or the Gullah world that largely replaced it. Many of the planters' mansions were burned during the Civil War, and others have since burned or fallen into decay. Slave quarters and the quaint shanties that followed them as well are gone. Cotton rows still make faint indentations, but forest has taken over. If we want to see what once was, a visit to Beaufort with a trip over to the Penn Center Museum is the best bet.

As resilient as ever, the Sea Islands have entered a new age. From the earliest colonial days, deadly fevers were a problem, and settlers sought summer sanctuary in seaside communities. They thought the sea air healthful, but actually the sea breeze was keeping away the mosquitoes that carried malaria and yellow fever. Best-known of these retreats was Sullivan's Island, but there were others—Edingsville, Rockville and even Beaufort—and around them grew up a tradition of vacation pleasure that bore fruit in this century.

As the original inhabitants were abandoning the islands, newcomers arrived. The public works projects of the New Deal meant roads and bridges. And in their wake entrepreneurs were quick to subdivide the oceanfront property. Then more inland land was settled. Golf courses replaced cotton fields. Fisherman and boats meant docks and marinas. The last half of this century has seen an amazing transformation of these islands; amazing in part because it has done so little to physically alter the landscape. Most developers were quick to recognize that the semi-tropical lushness of the re-emerging forest was best left intact.

But as with the geology of the Sea Islands, it's dangerous to generalize. Some of the islands have probably been overdeveloped, and some have not been developed at all. Some, like Bulls Island and Pinckney Island, are wildlife refuges. Some, like James Island, are traditional suburbs. Some, like Wadmalaw Island, are strictly agricultural. In out-of-the-way corners Gullah communities still exist, and the arts of this culture enjoy a revival. And practically every remaining plantation house has been restored. What goes unchanged, truly unchanged, though, what is most permanent about the Sea Islands, is the course of the warming Gulf Stream and the roll of the gentle waves and the shifting of all that sand. The Sea Islands are, after all, a gift from the sea.

Originally published in *South Carolina Wildlife* magazine

The Land Comes First: Robert Marvin

Robert Marvin was considered by many to be the South's most influential landscape architect. A half-century ago, he worked with Charles Fraser to set the development standards for Hilton Head Island, and the nature-based aesthetic he devised influenced all that followed.

Not long after Mrs. Whaley and her Charleston Garden *came out, I talked to him about doing a similar book. Sad to say, that didn't happen. However, in 2001, I did do this short interview. Robert had been very ill. In fact, our first appointment was canceled when he was sent into the hospital's intensive care unit. But once home, he urged me to come by. I was supposed to stay for ten minutes and stayed two hours, hours in which he spoke with great enthusiasm about how his wife and he had spent their lives—and about his love for the land. We parted. Then as I was backing the car from his drive, I heard my name called out. Robert was standing in the doorway, a bent, frail man, but one still capable of a broad smile.*

"Remember, Billy," he said. "The land comes first."

He died the following week.

When my wife, Anna Lou, and I came back here after school (in the late '40s), we had an idea that someday the South would get rich enough to mess itself up. We in the South had a wonderful landscape and there were people with the right values and work ethic, the right morals to preserve it—if given the chance. And you know the South in my lifetime has had that wealth come, and if we hadn't planned, our corner of it would have been ruined like so much of the rest of this country.

I'm happy to have stayed right here, to have not expanded with the company beyond the South. We could have gone to England. We even turned down an opportunity in Dallas. Ego would have been the only reason for leaving. I didn't care about making money. The land was what mattered—the doing good.

To design badly is a sin. (Oh, almost a sin.) You look to the site, design to the land. A landscape architect should be on every team and have powers equal to the architects. But back then this wouldn't have happened in the South—or outside of it very often. We weren't producing any Thomas Jeffersons in this country. Life had gotten way too complicated. People suffered from tunnel vision. When I got out of school in the late '40s, architecture and landscaping students weren't prepared to accept such a vision either—this ability to see and do the whole thing.

Before World War II, anything built, anything from a privy on up, was usually built better than it had to be. Projects were approached as important. After the war, that was changing. People were in a bigger hurry and they were losing contact.

What Charles Fraser says, "Whales were planned by God to live in the ocean," is true. Look at it this way. Man and woman were built by God to live in a garden. Therefore cities should be gardens. Even corporate high rises should be gardens, which is going to require a new kind of architect, a new form of architecture.

My grandfather planted a thousand acres of rice. And at the end of the day, he needed a cave to go into. His house, most plantation houses, were just boxes. Some had big windows, some were quite impressive, even beautiful in their way, but still they were boxes. The technology of his age had cut out all the rhythms of nature. We, today, need to be conscious of the sun. We need to knock down those walls and let the light in. Our emotional well-being and that of our kids and grandkids should be tied to nature. I can't say my grandfather needed this. He was outside every day all day long. He was trying to raise crops. He was in an adversarial relationship with nature. But that's behind us now.

I grew up on a plantation. On Bonny Donne over by Ritter. They had a garden designed there by the famous landscaper Umberto. This was a big place, a hunt club. When I went to catch the school bus, I was driven seven miles. I probably learned more from the Black man driving me that seven miles than from anyone else in my life. I learned more about being a human being. My father was the manager. I had six brothers and sisters. We all went to college. I got a degree in horticulture from Clemson, then went to the University of Georgia for an art degree, but didn't graduate. I didn't make good grades, but still I came away with a vision of what landscaping entailed. So once out of school, beginning around 1955, I began to educate myself. I knew little about art. But I knew art and not science should be the basis of my business. For three solid years, I read and talked to people, and I began to understand the principles of design, to understand color, form and texture.

I saw how simple it was to get a house to blend in—to put a couple of trees in front. I had a talent. Now the Bible says you can't serve two masters. Consider an art object. It has a dominant element. I couldn't make money and be the best landscaper that was possible. My wife wrote us a motto. "Robert Marvin and Associates' goal would be to create an environment in which each individual could develop into a full human being as God intended him or her to be."

The word environment—I don't think I'd ever heard it spoken in South Carolina. But in 1962, my wife and I drove in our Volkswagen out to a conference on the environment in Aspen, Colorado. We didn't have the money to fly. Two thousand people from all around the world showed up; Jonas Salk and others led. Artists, businessmen, scientists—every discipline was represented. Ten days spent there in this huge orange tent on the side of a mountain, the orange tent in a field of wildflowers and standing against the blue background of the sky. They spoke of how Americans could only react to their physical environment—to the material world. But their emotional environment was what affected their happiness, and they didn't even know how to talk about it. They lacked the vocabulary. Before that I'm not even sure I'd heard the word ecology spoken outside of a classroom. We came home invigorated.

And since then we've been studying, traveling, working—coming out of the "tunnel." I understood that an individual was the product of two forces, the God-given characteristics that made them special and the environment that surrounded him. And that environment should allow him to grow in every positive way possible. This is true for a house. It's true for the center of a city, and in the past decade much of my work has been in cities.

But how does a designer begin? If it's a residence, he goes to visit the family. You visit the kids. Three kids equal three personalities. Plus the parents. Two more personalities. They become a part of you. To be precise, you bond. Then you get out on the land. You have five different maps to reflect vegetation, slopes, soils, physical characteristics and is there noise? Where are the neighbors? How does the sun move? Mark all the trees. You build with the land. You don't cut the trees. Develop a house suited to the site, not vice versa. The land comes first.

The plantation today? I've spoken already of the need to let light into the house. To abandon that adversarial relationship with nature—that was my farming grandfather's lot. All day long he fought an unpredictable nature. We have it still with us today, that insecurity that requires man to dominate nature and retreat at night into a box. But not the justification. The gardens and immediate grounds can be considered in the same light. The live oaks, the camellias and azaleas, they harmonize. The oak avenues are classical—an ordering. You know, it's hard to talk about the emotional needs that a garden involves. In Europe with king and queen, you had a hierarchical world. Everything was formal, walled in. Trees got moved. Boxwoods got clipped. Then William Kent jumped the fence and discovered that all nature was a garden. Arts went informal then. And for a democracy like America, that should have been the answer. But in those early days we were in a wilderness, and emotionally there was usually a need for control in the garden, for trimming and geometrical security. Again, I think we have passed that.

In the Lowcountry, the wealth has always been in the plantations. In the beginning, rice was king. And indigo and cotton came along. But the Civil War ended that. General Sherman burned every house around here. By the time of the Depression, all the plantations had gone broke. The people who owned them might stay on as superintendents—my father was one. But at least the new owners cared about the land and they had the money to maintain it. Then in more recent years, the plantations were being sold once more. They were too expensive to maintain or the next generation had lost interest. Timber companies were buying them. But some property owners continued to care. Ones like Gaylord Donnelley, a wonderful man who fell in love with the land. He said, "I can't let this be destroyed." He invited the governor to go duck hunting. He involved people, and the result is the ACE Basin project—easements that preserve. Just remember. The land comes first.

Originally published in *Lowcountry Plantations Today*

Mama

It should be obvious that storytelling can have a cathartic element. People often tell stories because they must, and often those are the "best" kind to listen to. Heaven is a Beautiful Place *started out as an oral history collection of ghost stories, but Genevieve "Sister" Peterkin, with some gentle nudging from Patty Fulcher (who'd been transcribing the tapes), turned the book into a meditation on loss and love—and on courage. Here Sister talks about her mother Genevieve (who's own oral histories I'd read ten years before). The sentences that end the chapter preceding this one read: "Oh, but tears are so important. Memories can make you cry. You can even cry for joy. Sometimes it just comes to me—I'm really finally crying."*

MY MAMA, GENEVIEVE WILLCOX CHANDLER, was the only White woman around Murrells Inlet who would catch stone crabs with just her bare hands. You have to put your arm down in the hole. A stone crab is a bit like a lobster. The body is only four or five inches across, and it has one small claw. And it has one giant claw that can be as big as the rest of the crab put together. Now, we have five feet of tide along here. At high tide the water rises and the creek brims over and leaves just the tip of the marsh showing. At low tide the water falls, leaving the mudflats and oyster banks exposed and glistening. This is when you gather oysters and clams—and stone crabs if you have the courage.

Mama could take them, but it was the one thing I wouldn't even try. She told me exactly how, but I just wasn't brave enough. A stone crab makes a long tunnel down into the oyster rock, and this tunnel is well below the water level at that dead low tide. You can see the fresh shell that the old stone crab breaks off all around the entrance, and he is waiting at the bottom of that tunnel. This tunnel is always about an arm's length long, and what you do—I mean an expert does this but I can't—is you make your hand very stiff and keep your fingers very stiff. You start and run your hand right along the roof of the hole, and when you feel his back it's going to feel very smooth. He's always facing forward with his giant claw tucked up in front. You feel his back, you crook your fingers over it and then you snatch him quick. Or he gets you.

But if you snatch quick enough, that's all there is to it. He's out of the hole. You break off the big claw and let him go, and the little claw will grow to be the dominant one. But if you mess this up he can easily break one or more of your fingers, and there are even nightmare stories of people being held with their arms in the hole until the rising tide drowns them. And Mama did get bitten one time. She said she was lucky because the claw caught her in the fleshy part between the thumb and forefinger and her brother Dick was with her. She said that he said, "Sis, just relax, just relax, keep still and relax." So she lay there stretched out on the oyster rock with her arm down in the hole for quite a while and finally she felt the crab release her. She snatched her hand out, and Bubba Dick said if you don't go back and get that crab you'll never do it again. He made her stiffen her hand and go right back in and catch that animal. I suppose "make" isn't the right word. He encouraged her. He made her understand that if she didn't face her fear right then she probably never would.

Mama had actually grown up in Marion, South Carolina, which is a pretty little town about sixty miles in from the coast, but her father had discovered Murrells Inlet, which he rightly called "the Garden of Eden." He would bring his family here to vacation, and finally they settled permanently and were living in an old plantation housed called the Hermitage. When she was fourteen, Mama went off to a little Presbyterian college in North Carolina, Flora MacDonald, and after two years there she spent two years at the Art Students League in New York. Then she came home.

Mama was eighteen when her parents moved here to Murrells Inlet. The following year she started teaching school in nearby Collins Creek. She rode horseback from the Hermitage to that school, where she taught all eight grades in one classroom. She was the only teacher. She told me she always carried a pistol. Mama was very good with a rifle, but she always carried a pistol through that six miles of wilderness. She said the only thing she was afraid of were rattlesnakes and drunk men. She never had to shoot anything but a rattlesnake.

I heard a tale of those days not so long ago. Herman Wilson told his daughter he'd never forget his first day of school with Miss Genevieve. Mama was quite petite, and even the sixth grade boys were taller than she. Mr. Wilson said that first day Miss Genevieve came down the aisle, turned and faced them, reached in her pocket, and took out a pistol, which she laid on the desk. "Now, boys," she said, "I know I won't have any trouble with you this year." I expect she was just getting the word out that she was armed.

But once she did say that the meanest thing she ever did in her life was at that Collins Creek School. A creek ran right by the school windows, and she couldn't keep the boys' attention because a mother deer with a little spotted fawn was drinking from the creek or some other wildlife distraction was going on outside. She knew those boys were dreaming of hunting so she took a bucket of paint and painted over the glass in the lower half of all the windows.

I know she made a big difference in those children's lives, but she also realized pretty quickly that many of these children's parents were illiterate. White people, of course. A totally White school. Mama decided to go back at night and teach the parents, and her mother rode with her. They used a buggy at night. Mama said Granny would make coffee and doughnuts and haul them to the school. Mama said people came for refreshments and stayed to learn a little. And they did make a difference. They truly did. Sixty years later when I worked in the polls an amazing number of people told me they didn't have to make a mark for a signature. They'd say, "I can sign my name 'cause your mama taught me how." And some of the people who said that were Black, because during the same period Mama was doing adult education for Blacks in the kitchen of the Hermitage.

Another project that Mama and Granny undertook back then still gets occasional mention today. Around 1912 they put on what might have been the first outdoor drama ever staged on the East Coast. To make money for a school playground Granny took Longfellow's poem *Hiawatha* and wrote a script. All winter long the local families, both children and parents, came to the Hermitage. Granny gave out the speaking parts early so the actors could be studying, and the rest were sewing costumes. All the tin foil out of men's cigarette packages got saved to make glitter for the costumes. Also they used seashells. Basically, the seamstresses were decorating croker sacks. When *Hiawatha* was finally put on, people were amazed. Mama had an uncle who was a railway attorney and often traveled. He said, "Genevieve, how in the world did you find a costume house in New York to do all this?" Quite a compliment.

They always gave the play on the full moon in June because they needed the light of the moon and they needed the high water. In the end Hiawatha sailed away in his canoe. Men and boys hid out on a little shell midden and held onto a cable that ran inshore to the canoe. Hiawatha could just step into that canoe, raise his arms in the air, and glide out with the full moon in the background because the men and boys were gently tugging him out. One old man always told Mama how much he resented the *Hiawatha* production because his family—wife and children—would be at the Hermitage every Friday night working on that play. And confusing the Indian name with the setting, he'd call it "that damn old 'High Water.'"

In 1913 Mama went to Liverpool, England, and studied portrait painting. Then she returned home again and taught school until we entered World War I. The YWCA selected two young women from every state to send overseas, and Mama was chosen and attached to the Rainbow Division. Colonel Monroe Johnson, who also grew up in Marion, was her dear friend and commanding officer. Of course, Mama was a civilian. They were called YWCA Hostesses and were a forerunner of the Special Services, the same group I was a librarian with after World War II. She was stationed first in France and then in Germany during the occupation. They made and served doughnuts and coffee for the men, wrote letters for them and arranged for money orders to be sent home to wives, and that sort of thing.

Both her brothers were already over there with the Rainbow Division, and my father was with that division as well, but he didn't meet Mama until after the war. I don't know that Mama actually saw much of Europe. The hostesses weren't given much opportunity to tour. Once she attended a big dinner in a castle in Cologne, and that impressed her. And she saw General Pershing in Paris. When I was a child she still had her uniform, with its beautiful rainbow patch, but that disappeared somewhere along the line.

But long before the war Mama had been out in the world. She'd spent those two years in New York in the Art Students League. She had a professor there named Dumas who was quite famous, and if he felt your drawing was perfect he would initial it with a D on the bottom—a way of saying he wouldn't be embarrassed to claim it for his own. The year was 1910, and this was figure drawing. She did all these beautiful charcoal drawings and all were nude—both men and women. She must have been really shocked as a young woman to arrive from a little Presbyterian college like Flora MacDonald where they were still studying Gaelic and John Calvin—to go from that to New York and sketching the nude models.

Those sketches were in the attic at the Hermitage, and my sister June is a cleaner. I'm a clutterer. When June was around twenty she married. And she married a Yankee, which only made her worse about cleaning house. Her husband Ken was a wonderful man. I can honestly say that he and my sister, June, were and will always be two of my closest friends, but Ken and June together would go around like a whirlwind and whirl until they had established order. They cleaned up the attic. I guess June was twenty-one and I was eighteen, and I just knew this was a tragedy, but I couldn't stop them because they were "cleaning up." Letters and God knows what else beside those sketches with the D's on them—those two just pitched them into a bonfire in the yard. I was snatching out Mama's drawing as the flames were curling the white paper up, turning brown. And they were laughing and throwing the sketches back. I suppose the "cleaners" in life do have a point in that you can sink under the weight of all this nostalgia, but that really was a tragedy. Cleaning is something that should never happen to an attic, but if you couple a house-cleaning woman to a Yankee that's just what will happen.

Now, Mama again. She also played the piano, the organ and the violin. And she wrote fiction. A month before Daddy died she'd sold her first story to *Scribners*, and she sold five more to popular magazines before she stopped. These all dealt with Southern Black life—realistic portrayals similar to the ones my mother-in-law Julia Peterkin had done ten years earlier. And they sold for about twenty-five dollars apiece, so if she'd continued perhaps she'd have made a living as a writer.

I guess, before ending, I should also say that Mama was a pretty woman—beautiful really. But besides that she had a certain pride, an assurance about who she was. She carried herself well and tried to dress accordingly, and in this last wish she had help from some wonderful friends in Philadelphia. She met these two women at the Kimbels' and they'd send her boxes of fashionable clothes that they'd been wearing themselves only a few years earlier. This did make for a strange comparison when she was out working. I remember a picture taken of her in a black suede hat with a suede feather and a suede suit, interviewing Ben Horry, who was wearing rags with patches over patches. But I also remember a day in the Freewoods when Mama had on black lace stockings. A Black woman admired them and said, "Miss Genny, I'd give anything for stockings like that to wear to church on Sunday." My mama just hiked up her dress and rolled them off her legs and handed them to the woman. And when my little brother Bill was supposed to be Davy Crockett in a third grade play, Mama took the coonskin collar off this gorgeous coat from the North and the local seamstress made him a coonskin hat. And even more of the dresses got cut down for June and me, which was also a common practice among our neighbors. I remember one really poor little girl on the playground wearing beautiful velvet dresses with lace collars. She had to go barefoot, but the family had a rich relative in the North sending dresses. By the end of the war June was working, and if she bought a sweater for herself she'd buy one for me and something for the boys, and when I got a job I followed suit. Then by the1950s we could buy Mama clothes too—nothing like she'd worn in the 1930s, but at least suitable for her job.

June and my two youngest brothers inherited Daddy's blue eyes and blond hair. Tommy and I inherited Mama's dark hair and brown eyes. But what all five of us inherited from Mama—I should say what I hope we all inherited from Mama—was that pride I spoke of. I don't mean pride in being a Chandler, though, of course, we were. And not arrogant pride like the Flagg family were supposed to be guilty of. What I hope we inherited was Mama's pride in being what she was and what she expected each of us children to become—a brave and loving adult human being.

Originally published in *Heaven is a Beautiful Place*

The Art of Turnip Truckdom

I'LL TAKE MY STAND. THERE are a lot of topics around—collapsing savings and loans, collapsing universities, donkey basketball—on which I have skillfully walked the rail or else mumbled "no comment" while hiding my face behind a raised lapel. There is one subject, though, that I'm willing to stand up and be counted on. I like folk art. Correction. It's officially called "outsider art" now, but I like it all the same and so do a lot of other red-blooded Americans. I seem to remember Dwight Eisenhower chuckling the phrases of Grandma Moses, a saintly woman whose life and art were relatively typical (or used to be) of the genre. She started painting late in life and was self-taught. She had no sense of perspective, used bright colors and celebrated a nostalgic or naive, or at least pleasant, view of her surroundings.

I realize such generalizations are dangerous, but I'm taking my stand so I'll live dangerously. Grandma Moses was a typical folk artist (or used to be? maybe? many say? for her time?). Times change, of course. I still like Ike and I assume most other people do too, but folk art is no longer a matter to be left in the hands of benign Sunday painter presidents. It's big business, and it's social statement and still some of it's being painted right down the road by elderly grandparents. The medium is the message, and the message is, well...

My wife and I live in a small Southern rural town, and we grew up knowing personally a half-dozen such artists. Their paintings were the butt of some familiar jokes—as in the blazing sunset that was interpreted, "My God! Aunt May, you've painted the bomb!" But by and large this body of work of not-quite-right sailboats, magnolia blossoms and whatever was praised, appreciated and hung on the wall. It was the product of people who were known and loved—i.e., folks.

My wife and I didn't just fall off the turnip truck. We've been riding along on it now for a goodly number of years, knee-deep in turnips and peering out through the slats at a world we didn't make and have no desire to remake. Still and all, we're cosmopolitan enough to know the difference between Jasper Johns and Casper the Friendly Ghost. Plus, our son, a generation further removed from the Scottish Stone Age, is completing a degree in fine arts, and when he passed through his folk art phase, it was necessary as doting parents to flip through a handful of folk art paperbacks. We picked up a few points here and there, but even without this continuing education, we'd have stopped. In our travels in the greater realm of turnip truckdom, we'd never run away from a folk art exhibit, and weren't about to start now. Which brings us to Clayton, Georgia, and several summers back.

We'd just spent a week in the Blue Ridge Mountains and after enjoying a leisurely, white-knuckled, seven-hour drive along the parkway, we were fortunate enough to arrive in Clayton. Fortunate just to arrive anywhere, actually. And where did we find ourselves but in the midst of a month-long folk art exhibit spread out over three galleries. Before dark we reached the first of these and met a genial Atlanta art dealer, who sold us a crude little painting done by the daughter of a famous Florida "root carver." Just four slabs of white paint with pink blobs for heads, yellow smudged halos and some Christmas tree-like decorations for the borders, this little icon hangs in our living room now. And small world. Paying with a check, we discovered that the dealer's ninety-six-year-old grandmother had been born and raised at the lighthouse just off from our home and had been very close to my wife's family. Surely a good omen. We took heart and checked into the Clayton Hotel. In the morning we'd visit the other galleries to see the "Finsters."

Finster, of course, is Howard Finster, certainly the most famous folk artist alive. A former north Georgia evangelist, he has painted album covers for a rock group and taken commissions from the Coca-Cola Company. A Finster recently sold sight unseen for twenty-five thousand dollars. He doesn't do it for the money though (he really doesn't). He paints to spread God's word, and every painting is packed with the north Georgia equivalent of John Bunyan imagery and often-lengthy hand-lettered morals, admonitions and Scripture.

The next morning we were waiting when the Main Street Gallery opened. No Finsters in immediate sight, but the window was filled with the whimsical work of A.E. Miller. Painted on sheet metal, these showed Indians fighting dinosaurs and such other oddities. What's more, unlike the few Finsters inside, these were affordable. At least they would have been, except the proprietor told us they were hording Millers in Atlanta so they'd decided not to sell theirs. I asked her what was the difference between hording in Atlanta and not selling in Clayton? She said if it was up to her we could have one but her partners said no.

The last gallery was several miles out of town on the grounds of an artists' and writers' retreat. Here we were to find the bulk of the Finsters and could probably get a Miller sold to us. Maybe. The grounds were covered with curious whirly-gig-dinosaur weather vanes with propellers, but the gallery was closed. I wandered around back and into a second-floor music room where a man sat at a desk writing. He kindly offered to let us in. Walking back I asked if he was a musician, and he said he was a philosopher from a university in Virginia. He'd been writing philosophy. I told him I had just spent the week in the mountains with my friend Jack. Jack was also a philosopher but he hadn't written any in at least twenty years. In fact, he rarely mentioned philosophy. The Virginia philosopher asked me what Jack said when he did mention it, and I told him that once Jack had said, "Under certain circumstances anyone is capable of killing his wife." The Virginia philosopher thought about this a good thirty seconds and then agreed. He said, "He's right. Under certain circumstances anyone is capable of killing anyone else."

Now, I'm not including this bit of conversation to suggest the sad permissiveness to which Southern philosophy studies have sunk. Nor am I including it because it gave my wife (overhearing it from the far side of the still locked door) a few curious if not downright anxious moments. I'm including it because this was all it took to distract me from the fact that we'd entered from the back door and just walked through the entire exhibit. The art wasn't commanding our attention. It wasn't jumping off the wall screaming "admire me" or "buy me" or anything else.

We let my wife in, and though I could tell the Virginia philosopher wasn't a fan, he was good-natured enough to hang around while we browsed. Howard Finster predominated, God's word made flesh, so to speak. Familiar. I'd managed to visit an early Gothic cathedral once, and the enthusiasm of its earlier paintings and stained glass didn't seem to go so far removed from what the Georgia evangelist was attempting. Indeed, the angular, one-dimensional disciples and saints could even pass as distant cousins. Still, architecture aside, the cathedral art was so much more compelling—the promises so much more promising—that you wondered if the message was the same. No matter how clever and joyous the work of Howard Finster is (and it's both), the idea that a glimpse of Elvis and a Coca-Cola are among the primary rewards of both this world and the next do little to comfort this poor sinner.

Another artist represented, Mose Tolliver, was also known to me, at least from books. One of his paintings, "Man on Scooter," I'd seen reproduced.

Here was the original for a few hundred dollars. You could see the man and you could see the scooter. Maybe a few dozen dabs of paint in all. It was a strange, funny little muddle, but I couldn't help recalling a visit to the Tate Gallery. Van Gogh's sunflower paintings may be over publicized and overpriced but they are capable of dominating an entire gallery wall. "Man on Scooter" was barely holding down a few square inches. On the other hand, the artist wasn't charging thirty-something million either. In the rapidly escalating folk art market Toliver is still considered a very good buy.

But we were looking for a real bargain and got one. Yes, an "unhorded" A.E. Miller for a very modest sum. It's a squat sheet metal Uncle Sam with the words "Oscar Blows" on top of his head. Miller has a friend Oscar who drives into his yard and blows the horn—an act that's inspired dozens of these "Blow, Oscar, Blow" creations.

That was it. Goodbye, Clayton, Georgia. Hello, McClellanville, South Carolina. I'm told "Oscar Blows" is now worth three times what we paid, so in another year we'll have salvaged the price of the hotel room. Good. That's about as far as I want to get involved in the business end of folk art. And "Oscar Blows" is about as much social commentary as I'm up to. In fact, though we were happy with him and the four angels, I still feel a bit guilty about carrying them across state lines. This may be celebrating the rural Southern experience, but my wife and I are not directly connected to the lives of these painters. Their community is not ours, nor is their adventure. While these paintings certainly didn't depend on this level of intimacy to succeed, I couldn't help thinking we were buying (at a cut rate) what should be a very personal form of expression.

And that brings us to Captain Joe Cumbee. I'd gotten this far in this essay and then set it aside waiting for the white heat of inspiration to spur me to a conclusion. None came, but then a friend called from the state museum to tell me that my old buddy Captain Joe had received South Carolina's Heritage Award. Only four craftsmen are selected each year, and far as she knew Joe was the first folk artist ever to win. My museum friend was excited about this and so was I, for we both recognize that Captain Joe is the real thing.

My first job out of graduate school (many years ago) was to work with this retired tugboat captain as a "ship's carpenter," which is a rather exacting discipline Joe administered almost completely with a yard axe. Widowed sometime before, he'd recently remarried, an occasion happy enough to renew his interest in painting, and he'd showed me several works. Since I'd just been studying the surrealists for a year and a half and had a degree, I felt qualified enough to tell him he was a very good artist and could probably even make a living at it. He shrugged off this compliment, went shrimping next and then back to running an ocean-going tug. He'd made his last trip while going well into his seventies; a barge load of Christmas trees to Venezuela.

A premonition told him the aging tug wouldn't survive another such voyage. It didn't, but by then he was home for good, home puttering and drinking black coffee.

I'd been told to give the state a week to notify him of the award and then I could go out and congratulate him myself. Short trip. He only lives five miles away, but to my shame, I hadn't seen him in two years. At his trailer, I find little has changed. He's seated in a living room piled high with clutter, watching TV and drinking black coffee. "Old Billy Baldwin," he keeps repeating. "Where you been?" Good question. The walls are lined with paintings, at least half of them his. I remember most. The houses of his make-believe seaside communities shrink from the canvas in curious cubist distortions, but the boats are always perfectly proportioned. He's laughed many times about his failure to make the transition from sea to land. There are only two new works, drawings in colored pencil of a local landmark, Deer Head Oak. He's drawn from memory. The oak tree limbs climb to the sky in thick green intertwining arms. Not limbs or even antlers. Not a live oak. Maybe an exotic boab growing at least two continents away. He tells me the first tree wasn't right because there were no children playing in it. The second drawing corrected that. In the corner the TV still runs. A talk show where the topic for the day is nudity in the home. Naked parents are wandering around in front of naked children in suburban America. Joe has drawn clothes on the tree children.

I sip my coffee and congratulate him on being one of the state's Heritage winners. He hasn't heard the news and asks me what it means. I say that I guess it means he's one of the best folk artists in South Carolina. For this year, at least, one of the very best. He smiles and says, "I'll be dog gone."

That's his response in total. He hasn't painted or even drawn in months. "I'm eighty-three years old," he says. "My eyes don't see. My hands don't go where I tell them." But even as he says this his thick fingers cut the air between us—an act of pure expression I've been observing for a quarter of a century and one I assume is far older. Joe told me once that he'd started painting on sail canvas with white lead for gesso. That puts his career back to the age of sail when he was a fourteen-year-old-cabin boy on a rum-running schooner. On this visit, though, I ask just how long he has been painting. He answers, "All my life."

"Old lady Peacock. She told me I could draw. She meant well but I didn't know it then. Wouldn't let go of me. I quit school just to escape old lady Peacock." He's talking about the fourth grade.

On the TV a game show flashes. Blinking lights and a promise of a life far away filled with chrome-plated mechanical garbage. We only stop to watch when this frenzy is occasionally interrupted by a stern-faced reporter announcing the latest of Iraq's sadly belated attempts to surrender. The captain and I are catching up. We discuss old times and new times, everything, in fact, but art. Finally that too. He says, "All my grandchildren want to draw. My great-granddaughter drew this one." He slides the paper toward me. "Said 'It's a boat, Granddad. It's a boat.'"

Indeed, it is a boat. A high-bowed craft with a narrow two-story cabin well forward. One round window and one square. Centered on the deck, a squiggly mast flying a single lopsided pennant. It's a bit too sketchy to identify the exact boat depicted, but the impulse to create is familiar enough. And a child's unsteady hand has printed across the bottom, "I LOVE YOU." So, that's that. Or to quote the master, "I'll be dog gone."

What did I leave out of this? The last barge load of Christmas trees, the ones Captain Joe refused to haul, washed up on the shores of Venezuela. The tug was never heard from again. Joe said a premonition told him to get off the boat, but he also said the metal of that tug's hull was rusted so thin you could stick a pocket knife blade through it. That's how he knew for certain it was time to find another berth—or better yet, retire.

Smallest of all possible worlds: the mother of the folk art dealer in Clayton was Ingra, the light keeper's daughter, who gives the account of growing up on Bulls Island (you'll find it in the lighthouse essay). As a child, Captain Joe also spent time on Bulls Island, but that would have been about ten years later. He told me that during the 1911 hurricane, he remembered the water coming up around the Magwood house where they were all staying. The adults had discussed which kind of tree was best to tie the children up in and settled on palmetto. They were easing out the door to see to this chore when the water began to recede. He was five at the time.

Originally published in *Chronicles*

Martha and Jay Go to Oregon

Martha and Jay Shuler grew up in McClellanville and spent much of their adult lives on the shores of Bulls Bay. Jay ran the Bulls Island ferry for seven years and was known to birders (those are bird watchers) throughout the country. He took the last photograph of a Bachman Warbler. And for twenty years his nature photography was used extensively in Southern schools. He was responsible for the preservation of the I'On Swamp tract in Awendaw—today, one of the most visited spots on the coast. By their lives and "teachings" Jay and Martha influenced us all.

Jay and Martha weren't childhood sweethearts. But Jay did let the younger Martha follow him when he went into the woods exploring. The day he stopped to hold up a barbwire fence for her, she knew he cared. She was sixteen. Jay went off to WWII and finished Clemson and then they were married. Martha was employed as a social worker but was continually confounded by bureaucratic restrictions. Jay had had an unhappy year as a schoolteacher and after that sold "burial insurance." And then…

FOUR YEARS WE'D BEEN MARRIED, and one day Jay came home and said, "Let's start over. We're not getting anywhere. Let's go to Oregon. I can get a job there as a firewatcher."

So we both quit our jobs and took off. Mother looked so sad when she was waving goodbye. Later I asked her why and she said, "Because I thought I'd never see you again. But I knew you were happy and that was all that mattered."

This was 1952. For the trip to Oregon, Jay bought us an old Henry J. Kaiser car with four "new" recapped tires—tires that unraveled as we crossed the desert. Jay would cut the unraveling parts off with a razor blade. When we reached Oregon the head ranger of the forest asked, "You came all the way across the country with those tires?"

We said, "Yes." Immediately he bought us four new tires.

But that was at the end of the trip. In order to cross America we had bought a pup tent and air mattresses. Instead of sleeping bags we had army blankets supplemented with white linen sheets and pillow cases—wedding presents. And we had a little camp stove, an ice chest and a box for groceries.

We were so excited. We were going camping. This was 1952 and there were no campgrounds to speak of. We'd ask farmers if we could park under their trees and sleep. I'll never forget in Indiana we had permission from a farmer. We pitched our pup tent under his tree. But he was plowing his field at night. Forty acres I suppose. In the time it took him to circle the field, we'd go to sleep. Then as he returned the lights on his tractor would wake us. He'd stop and chat for a half hour. Then he'd go around again and we'd sleep for a while longer. A wonderful experience—the entire trip.

When we got to the Red Desert, it turned really cold and the wind blew so hard we had to clutch onto the tent to keep it from blowing away. And at Yellowstone we went to sleep snug in our tent, and as usual, our feet were sticking out the end, covered over with plastic—a polyurethane kind of plastic, which was new then. The first day of June and we woke up with a foot of snow mounded over our feet. A little cafe was opening up for the first time that summer, and we bought ourselves a meal, which was a great extravagance. We had dollar pancakes. Then we just sat inside the cafe and stayed warm for as long as we dared.

Finally, we got to Oregon. We were stationed inland, but drove to the ocean first. Seeing the Pacific I said, "You mean Oregon is on the coast?" That's how I learned geography. Hands on. In the years since, we've camped in every state except Hawaii and Alaska. But I must tell you of Oregon in 1952.

The forest service people were so very good to us. First we went to firewatching school for two weeks. I went too, because I was to be Jay's relief. Then we were assigned to the Drake Butte tower, which was high on a mountain at the end of an impossible road. One or the other of us were to be in that tower during the daylight hours seven days a week.

At ground level, a one-room log cabin with surrounding windows was under the spokes of the tower, and we were to keep watch for fires even from there. Inside were a woodstove and a small bed. Just us. We spent so much time alone together it was like a second honeymoon.

Not long after we got there, a letter came from Mother saying, "You've had the trip and now have to pay the price." Lord knows how my letter had given that impression. Jay and I whooped with laughter, and I wrote her back: "The 'price' is peace of mind and heart. We love it. You can't imagine waking up to a cool, brisk summer morning with the birds singing all around, the ground squirrels and chipmunks begging for their breakfast and miles and miles of rolling mountains for a view. Soon the fire is going in the friendly woodstove and the bacon and eggs smell like heaven. There's enough to do during the day to keep you busy and happy but no real worries. In the evening you walk around in the beautiful forest and stop to look for arrowheads, agates, or small wild flowers. You watch the sunset behind Mt. Jefferson and there's not another sight like it in this world."

Still, I wasn't telling her the complete truth. For one thing up there that summer, Jay and I were nudists. We didn't wear clothes unless we heard a truck coming up the road—and that was easy to hear. But one day I was up in the tower and Jay was down below completely naked and cutting wood. I had taken clothes up with me in case anybody came.

Well, I saw a rancher coming up on horseback and I yelled to Jay. This rancher stayed to visit a bit. We wanted to be hospitable so I learned to make upside down cake in the frying pan. Other ranchers started visiting, too. I'd serve cake and coffee. This was unusual. Usually the firewatchers were ignored. But they brought us venison and antelope and we were glad for the company.

On Saturdays and Sundays I had to go up in the tower. On the other days I would get up and start the fire in the woodstove and then carry the little gas heater to the outhouse that sat on the side of the mountain. Not quite like I'd told Mama, because even in summer it could drop to eighteen degrees at night. On the weekends Jay would tell me to stoke the stove and I'd push him out of bed—since "I" was on duty then.

On weekdays, I would sit outside with nuts, berries and the like in my hand. I'd just hold the food and sit absolutely still and animals would come. First I'd put it out on the rock and then moved closer. Finally I held the treat in my hand and the Clark's Nuthatches, scrub jays, other jays, even chipmunks ate from my hand, and little ground squirrels—like little people—and red squirrels.

When we'd first arrived, I'd shouted, "Jay, look at that! That is the most interesting bird." Of course, I'd never seen anything like those Western birds. But he said, "Mart, that's just a robin, a robin exactly like ours." I said, "Well, it surely does look different out here." These birds eating out of my hand really did look different, wonderfully exotic—and not one was a robin.

That summer I had the kind of leisure I've never had since. Jay would be in the tower. I'd bake my cake and wash the windows. After that there was nothing to do but read. I'd take my book, my *Moby Dick*, and sit on a rock. I'd feel that warm sun on my back and arms, forget about the reading and just gaze at the mountains. We celebrated our fifth wedding anniversary at that fire tower and life had never been so good.

The nearest town was Prineville. Close by but still several hours away. The roads were awful. With ruts a foot deep and boulders protruding, some of those roads were no more than glorified streambeds. Jay would drive to town one day a week to do our laundry and buy some groceries. Ordinarily I'd call in a grocery order and they'd send everything on Friday. But I hated to call in my grocery list. They laughed at my pronunciation (my Southern drawl) and when I ordered "hominy," meaning "grits," they sent canned hominy in lye.

Anyway, Jay had gone to town one Saturday and I was in the tower. Over the radio I heard somebody say, "Did you get Shuler out?" Somebody else said, "Shut up!" Of course, I called in and one of the rangers explained that Jay was coming home and stopped to take a photograph on the side of the road. "When he pulled back out," the man explained, "his tire was too close to the cliff and he sort of went down it. But he is all right. We got him out." The car slid down the cliff and rested against a tree. Jay climbed out the window and scrambled up to the road. He got home but he was awfully late.

Before we left home Jay had bought himself a decent camera, a Nikon, which he would use for the next twenty years.

And that accident at the cliff was how it would be from then on. Really. The worst accident he had was in Mexico. Climbing a tree to photograph a bird, he fell and broke his ankle. And a lot of the time the accidents weren't even accidents. Wherever we went Jay had a habit of lying down on the roadside on his belly to photograph tiny little flowers. Inevitably somebody would stop and want to know if they could help—for they assumed he needed first aid. And one man even said, "I'll help you get him back in the car and I've got coffee here."

We stayed on at the fire tower from early June until snow fell. That's how our contract read. But once the snow started we had to get off the mountain immediately. By then Mother was with us. At the end of July, I had started begging her to come and the first of October she'd arrived. She had flown out to see us and to make the trip home. We planned to stay in different parks.

We were already packed, but even so it got bad quickly. Just that narrow dirt road going straight up from the bottom of the butte. Jay was outside the car, holding it on the road with his hands and shoulder. I was steering the Henry J. and Jay was using his body to keep us from skidding and plunging to our death, and halfway down, Mother shouts, "Martha, you forgot your snake!" And I had. I'd forgotten my Pacific Rubber Boa that I always wore around my arm. It loved the warmth of me and was just the nicest snake. This was the one wild pet I would allow into the cabin and the only one I intended to take home. I'd punched holes in the top of a jar and had him in there. We really were attached to each other but being half way down the mountain, we had no choice but to leave him behind to freeze.

That trip home was made from park to park. We still didn't have any real camping equipment. We did use our ice chest and little stove to make meals, but Mama paid for motels all the way home. Except she only got one room. Mother and Jay loved to stay up all night and talk. Finally, one night, I said, "Mama, you just get in bed with Jay and I'll get in your bed. I can't sleep with you all talking and laughing all night long." Mama had such a good time on that trip. Daddy would never go anywhere but he was happy to send her. We went to the north rim of the Grand Canyon, Carlsbad Caverns—we went to every park we could.

That was Oregon. That was my first experience of just trusting Jay completely. I always had this dark vision. I worried about everything. But that trip changed our lives. I never felt the same about anything. I saw life was to be lived—to be experienced with joy. We—that is mankind—weren't meant to work nine to five. But if we had to, at least, we could pick jobs that allowed us the summers off. And that's what we did. After that, each summer we'd take off to Wyoming or the Blue Ridge Mountains. We'd go somewhere.

And sometimes we didn't even wait until summer.

Originally published in *The Nature of Beauty*

Ali Fulcher Shuler

I remember when Ali was born. Since she's twenty-eight, that's not so hard to do. Her mother, Patty Fulcher, and I have worked together on at least a half dozen projects. Her father, Jim Fulcher, is my doctor. I was looking for a "modern" take on Cape Romain and the rest of the Sea Island world, and since Ali had been teaching McClellanville students a course called "Salt Marsh," she seemed like the natural choice. Like Jay and Martha, she'd gone to Oregon at an impressionable age. In fact, this classroom she mentions first wasn't too far from their mountain watchtower.

I HATE THE WORD ENVIRONMENTALIST. Too many connotations. That really came home to me when I spoke at the Central Point high school near Ashland. This is southern Oregon. The school was in one of those little logging towns, the kind that were booming at their height and are shrinking now. The environmentalists (whoever they are) are credited with destroying these towns. But the big lumber companies like Boise Cascade were moving anyway. The mills were headed to South America and Canada, but environmentalists got the blame. The mills' public relations people did an amazing job.

I met the Central Point teacher (the one who threw me to the wolves) outside the little food cooperative in Ashland. I was getting signatures—we wanted people to come camp out, wanted them to actually experience a threatened forest. The teacher introduces himself and says, "I have a 10th grade class at Central Point. Come talk to them. My students will love it."

"What kind of slant would you like? Aim it how?"

"Whatever you want."

I said, "I'll talk about 'home.' This area is their home."

A week later I walked in the door of that classroom and he introduced me as "an environmentalist." He didn't say "militant environmentalist" but that was his intent. Then he explained that over the preceding week he'd had his students write about what they thought an environmentalist was—the kind of person. And he'd had them ask the same question of their parents.

When I first go into crowds I have on blinders. I don't look around. I'm focusing on the teacher and I'm feeling the tension in the room. Tenth graders. We're talking big old strapping logging boys who that summer had helped their daddies "fell the side of a mountain." And I look on the black board. There're headings written across the top: environmentalist and logger are the first two. Under environmentalist is written: Tree spiker, arsonist. One just has asterisks to represent the cuss words. I have my little slide show. I've come to talk about "home." It doesn't help to shake around kids. And now the teacher wants his students to talk about the interviews with their parents. He claims they haven't discussed these yet. He says they have certain stereotypes of environmentalists.

"Are they all negative?" I ask. Silly question.

I heard one boy shifting up in his chair. He grunts, "Yeah."

Cowboy boots. That's what I'd heard shifting. Lots of cowboy boots in the room.

The teacher says, "Mr. Bronson, what do your parents think of environmentalists?"

I know now where the asterisks probably came from.

This boy says, "I really can't repeat that in class." They all have this Southern accent. I think of it as Southern—twangy, drawn out. A country accent. He says that and grins and now all the kids are laughing at what he's said. So I start laughing. That confuses the teacher. He wants confrontation.

I give my slide show—which is pretty tame. I talk about basic ecology and about sense of place. And about prescribed burning. Out West they don't burn on a regular basis, so they have terrible wild fires. The kids all agree that fire is good. peregrine falcons are good. They all agree. Still, they all want to be able to do what they want in the forest. Don't tread on me. It's a matter of *rights.*

I don't agree with some multiple use issues. I'm against snowmobiles. And I don't like four wheelers, but at least those kids riding them are going in the forest. At least they are getting to know their "home." I tell them, "That's fantastic." I ask if they want clean water. Yeah. Do they want clean air? Yeah. Do they want healthy wild places to explore? Yeah.

I say, "Well, that is the definition of an environmentalist—someone who actively works for those goals."

It's absurd. We all want a healthy environment. We live inside it. All of us. We don't all work actively for that goal. I realize now that the best way to educate children is to simply take them out into an Oregon forest, out on a South Carolina marsh, and let them be a part of the natural world. Let them learn about the land. Let them wander it. Then they'll understand the importance of writing letters, making phone calls, of becoming involved in the protection of this gift they've been given—we've all been given. That's the simplest way to side step all those negatives, all the bad baggage that the word environmentalist carries.

Oregon? I could have stayed on in Oregon. But I was burnt out, tired of being a part of those tremendous organizations. And I felt too disconnected. Too disconnected from what was happening in South Carolina. Our coast is so vulnerable. I took this teaching job. The name of the course is "Salt Marsh." That's a pretty basic title and the course is just that—a basic introduction to what these kids have right in front of them. I want them involved in the future of the Cape Romain Wildlife Refuge. We have this tremendous salt marsh in front of us, miles of untouched beaches right there, and other reserves to the north and south. And I want them involved in the future of the Francis Marion National Forest. There's a quarter of a million acres of woodlands at our back.

Jay Shuler, and then after him my dad, were able to save thousands of acres in the Francis Marion Forest as Wilderness Areas. These pristine places were going to be cut, but they lobbied, they wrote letters to Congressmen and even went up to Washington. They had groups behind them, they had the threat of Sierra Club lawyers waiting in the wings, but they worked pretty much alone. They weren't members of some giant faceless environmental organization. And they accomplished an amazing amount. Whatever works. Whatever works works.

I just want my students to be involved. I want them to be out in the marsh, out in the forest, on the Sea Islands, in the creeks. Some are the sons and daughters of fishermen, the children of shrimpers. The situation is no different from that facing the children in that Oregon school, the children of those displaced loggers. I want my students to understand that this land around them is their home. I want them to "see" the land. And this really isn't something you can preach. Preaching—that very straight "scientific" mono—speaking just doesn't reach the students in the way that's needed. If you want to change people's minds you have to make them hungry for the wilderness. Somehow, you have to give them the whole experience. Let them see that this is the time for the mushrooms. Or the sulfur butterflies. It's time for this change and that. Let them experience the woods and marshes the way you experience a garden. Think of the light changes in the fall. The angle of the sun shifts and now this incredible light is reflecting off the browns and golds of the marsh grasses. To really "see" the natural world requires an investment of time—a great chunk of time. And with that investment comes familiarity. Familiarity leads to friendship. And finally, if they can begin to see the environment around them as an old friend instead of some alien other, if the very presence of the woods and marshes fills them with good memories—the rest is easy. You don't see until you relax.

Names and Places

I'D GRADUATED FROM TWO YEARS of crabbing to a small thirty-six foot shrimp boat, which I'd carried into the ocean with no experience whatsoever. In the Cape Romain waterways I bounced along half aground following in the wake of boats that I knew drew twice the water I did. While in the ocean, I dragged about oblivious to the fact that underwater wreckage waited at well-defined points to rip every mesh of webbing from the lines. And so, in the middle of the second week, I was following Gene Morrison's *Miss Edna* as she swung in behind the schooner hang and out again. I swung, too, but my boat was brought up short, and when I got the net back on board, it was only half a net. Late that afternoon Gene called and invited me around to his trailer. He had a net for me—a fifty-foot flat net that I could use, and even more valuable, he wanted to explain to me about ranges.

For most sailors I'm sure that the existence of ranges would come as no surprise, but I was a misplaced crabber and English major, ignorant of the world in general and the ocean in particular. I did have a chart or two, but the ranges he was to describe that afternoon were far more sophisticated and subtle than any man-made markers found at a harbor's entrance. To begin with, Gene explained, there was the basic triangle. I, standing at the wheelhouse, was one point of the triangle. A square bush (a tree) on Lighthouse Island would be the second point, and the big lighthouse, slightly behind, and to one side, formed the third. As I moved, my relationship to these other two points shifted. Depending on the triangulation involved, a range could be fast closing, or slow. The one he spoke of, the bush and the lighthouse was fast. It could be read from both south (the Sandy Point side), and north (the Santee side), and could be used depending on its positioning to warn you of several wrecks, or simply to "keep you on the shrimp."

That was in 1968, and there were only three Coast Guard-maintained buoys in the Cape Romain area. They marked the undredged, and often impassable, entrance to the Sandy Point Inlet. Most boats simply ignored "the cans," turned up the beach to a tremendous piece of driftwood dunnage called "the block," and headed off into the northeast until they could place the first of the Lighthouse Island woods on the lighthouse. The same type of reckoning brought you into the Santee's Northeast Point inlet—one even shallower than Sandy Point's and one entirely off limits according to the Coast Guard.

Only two shrimp boats had radar at the time, and the rest worked from ranges aided by depth finders and compasses. It was accurate, accurate enough for me anyway. Seven years later I was one of the few boats still operating without radar. By then I'd learned most, if not all, of the lone pine trees, pieces of driftwood, sand or shell banks, bushes, lighthouses, cans, islands, wood indentations and dips, that made up that ever shifting mosaic of coordinates and reckonings that told you were you were in the ocean, and the Cape Romain waterways, as well. By then I knew no landmark was too insignificant, and practically everything out there, whether mapped or not had a name. The two dimensions of the chart or map were transferred to a three-dimensional land of workday reality, which was how many of the creeks and islands on the charts had been named in the first place.

Three hundred years before, boatmen had begun to pass through Cape Romain's inland passage, leaving in their wake a collection of the most matter-of-fact descriptive names that could be imagined (or unimagined). Most were landmarks, ranges to sail by, others were simply sailing directions—directions concerning tide, wind and depth of water. But before we touch on that legacy, we must push back to the "very" beginning, to the naming of the Cape.

In 1526 Lucas Vasquez de Ayllon had set sail from Santa Domingo with five hundred men, as well as slaves, women and horses. Landing his settlers to the north at Cape Fear he marched them down the coast to Georgetown's Winyah Bay for settlement and in the process sighted Cape Romain from his ship on August 24. Since it was the Spanish custom to name a landfall after a saint's day on which it was discovered, (see St. Augustine and St. Helena) our Cape commemorates San Romanus, a disciple of St. Peter and a Tuscan bishop who had been martyred on that day. Maybe. The interpretations given to the meager, and inexact records are often in conflict and modern historians have shifted the site back and forth between Savannah and Cape Fear. In fact, Ayllon's latitude readings for his final settlement give the highly unlikely spot of Cape Romain's Murphy Island. And, of course if the settlement site shifts, then so does the Cape. And worse yet, modern Catholic scholarship has done away with our saint altogether. Anyway, Ayllon died and the few survivors returned to Cuba.

Though often confused with Cape Fear, Cape Romain would remain on the maps. This shoal was particularly dangerous to Spanish treasure fleets, which often came this far north before veering eastward. By 1666, Spanish influence was on the wane in North America and the English explorer, Sandford, renamed the landfall.

Sandford wrote, "I blotted out the name of St. Romaine putt before the next Easterly Cape, and writt Cape Cartrett in the roome, to evidence the more reall right of Sr. George Cartrett as hee is a hard Proprietor of Carolina."

Christened for his employer, the Cape would be labeled Cartarett on English maps until the proprietary government ended fifty years later. Then both proprietor, and saint would share the honor equally until the Revolutionary War, when, free from the English obligations, it was labeled—as mariners had probably continued to call it—Cape Romain.

As these early maps show, there was little official naming done during this first century. In about 1720 Indian fighter Barnwell had given the name of (Stephen) Bull to the island called by the Indians "Oneseau," but retained Sewee for what would soon be Bulls Bay. "Rockoone Island" was marked, and Murphy Island was named Bruneau for the Swiss who had planned, but failed, to build a windmill there.

On the mainland at McClellanville is the faint announcement of Linch. That's Lynch in later days and the only reminder we have that in the 1750s, Thomas Lynch, signer of the Declaration of Independence, was spending some of his boyhood at the family summer home on Raccoon Key.

It was not until 1771 that mapmakers Cook and Lodge drew a reasonable facsimile of the Cape Island, and added some significant information. "Freshwater at the low point," they wrote for ship captains attempting to judge the Santee River's entry. Plus a landmark for those early ships attempting to use the "Horns I[nlet]," an opening in the Santee Delta marked by two large horn-shaped dunes or sandbars.

Lynch's brother-in-law, Scotsman Bowman's survey added little to this. He drew crudely. He numbered his marsh holdings, and named only the one most important to him, Mill Island.

It was not until Robert Mills's map of 1825 that significant names were added, and the names he showed were usually just landmarks familiar to the boatmen passing through the area. "Horns," "Sand Island," "Mill," "Five Creeks," "White Banks," "Sandy Point," and on the far side of Bulls Bay, "The Mulberry" and "Peach Tree."

Robert Mills, for those who don't remember, was a South Carolinian and the United States' first native-born architect. A disciple of Thomas Jefferson, he designed many of the courthouses in the state and is best known for the Washington Monument in our nation's capital. But as a young man he had difficulty supporting himself and took work as South Carolina's principal engineer. As such he was responsible for the canals that were being built along the length of the state's coast—in the hope that Charleston's sagging economy could be improved.

The engineers that preceded Mills in 1818 had bothered to name nothing and instead had numbered the creeks that would be altered. Mills objected to this strongly. Not only did he use proper names while charting his course, he asked that when possible Indian names be retained. Of the Cape's, he managed to salvage only Jeremy Island, adding his own internal rhyme by spelling it "Jeremymy."

The idea may not have been completely original with Mills, for Washington Irving of "Rip Van Winkle" and the "Headless Horseman" fame had already written, "I have, on former occasion, suggested the expediency of searching out the original Indian names of places, and whenever they are striking and euphonious, and those by which they have been superseded are glaringly objectionable, to restore them." An example Irving gives is the replacement of the humdrum "Mill Creek" with the original "Pocantico."

By the standards of Mills and Irving, the Cape did poorly. We have Jeremy, a Sewee Indian king. But Oniseau is gone. Sewee Bay became Bulls Bay, with the Sewee getting a much smaller and shallower bay nearby. Awendayborough got shortened to Awendaw. Tibwin remains, and of course the Santee River, which may translate out to something like "there is the river." The rest of the Indian names have been lost along with any real understanding of the languages. Still, it can be argued that Mills was being too harsh, or at least unrealistic. The settlers, while reluctant to adopt a tongue-twisting destination like Awendayborough, were not without a certain sense of poetic wonder and a few of the names reflect this well enough. When Raccoon Key was named, a raccoon was a novel animal with a brand new name, an Indian name at that. It meant, "he scratches with his feet." Explorer John Lawson, who passed our way in 1700, expanded on this considerably, telling how the raccoon would fish for crabs by using his tail for bait. The same could be said for the mundane alligator of Alligator Creek. "El lagarto de Indias," lizard of the Indies, hadn't entered the language as "aligarto" until 1591. A mere hundred years later, Lawson wrote that they were harmless, but still managed to spin an exciting yarn filled with "roaring beasts." There were abundant raccoons on the islands and alligators filled the fresher creeks—but we shouldn't forget that what we take for granted might have excited the wonder of a new arrival—even the most common inhabitant of all. Oyster Bay would have held a culinary promise for hungry settlers that Mills and Irving might not have truly appreciated.

Mills's map, "the old map," would be used by the Union blocking forces, for preceding the war, the navy had surveyed only the major inlets. The first true survey of the inland waterways wasn't completed until 1887, at which time an effort was made to name most of what had officially been mapped. The coastal geodetic survey teams refined this work over the years, changed a few names and added a few more. That's what's being used today.

A few first names have found their way on at the end of the nineteenth century—Clark, Nellie, Joe and Ben, perhaps the children of local families or fishermen. The surnames DuPre, Skrine, Graham and Vanderhorst mark the creeks which once connected their mainland property to the outside world. The rest are names of necessity and convenience. Now here's an overview.

While we may celebrate or commemorate, the basic need for the earliest travelers was to recognize. When faced with a landscape of level expanses of marsh and water that some have unkindly labeled "monotonous" and all have referred to as a "labyrinth," it was essential to differentiate between the creeks and pick out channels through the shallow bays. Under these circumstances a low shell bank or a small bush could take on a truly monumental significance and be immortalized accordingly.

If we study the modern chart, we can easily pick out the trails, which the early canoes and schooners had followed while crossing from the Santee River to Charleston Harbor.

A traveler of this inland passage would have left Alligator Creek at Ramhorn Creek, then passed through the narrow Needles Eye and into Mill Creek, which carried him into Casino Creek. The original Cassena shore on which the cassena bush had grown in 1771 was washing away when I was a boy, but Yankee map markers had long since misunderstood the local pronunciation and converted the creek name to Casino. Turning right, our boatman would enter Congaree Boat Creek. (A reminder that the entire passage was called the Congaree Boat Creek or Santee Path or Pass because by following the Santee River, our traveler eventually reached the fall line of the Congaree just below Columbia). Next he would approach Horsehead Island, which was probably marked by a horse head-shaped bush or an actual animal's skull. The creek beside it is Cowhead. From there he crossed Muddy Bay, formerly Oyster Bay, and entered Papas Creek, which is the Gullah or Geechee pronunciation of Porpoise, and like Cassena had fallen victim to army engineers' transcribing. A turn down thirty-foot-deep Five Fathoms Creek would carry him past a "sandy point" toward the ocean or bay. A turn up Five Fathoms would take him through Five Creeks, through Bull River and then across the bay past White Banks, Vessel Reef and Bird Bank, out through Bull Channel, Bull Narrows and on to Charles Town, which was also Charleston.

There was, of course, an alternate route. At one time or another, almost all the creeks were part of the path, or inland waterway. In his explanation of the canal construction Mills had warned against the route that passed just in shore of the ocean. This way the schooner would turn right out of Casino Creek, cross Cape Romain Harbor passing Mill Den and Devil's Den. These dens twist and turn like an animal burrow, but I was taught by my Uncle Wewa Leland that a den was not an ordinary creek. It was one whose mouth could be confused on a dark night for a proper creek, or passage. Mill Den could be confused with Mill Creek and Devil's Den easily taken for Slack Reach, which comes next. A reach is a boatman's term for a straight stretch of water. Slack meant slack tide. The flood tides meet there. The mill of Mill Island was of course an obvious landmark, as were the two lighthouses, and passing there you traveled up Romain River either to Clark's Creek previously Schooner Creek or into Santee Path, which ran over into Sett, which was the original name for this entire stretch of water.

A "sett," I suspect, is really a set—a sail course or wind direction as most familiarly noted, "to set sail." A tack could be made into the prevailing southeast breeze here and, of course, a northeaster would speed things along. But a set is also an even more antiquated and obscure reference to the tides. The set of the tide was particularly important since most of this travel was conducted with the tide in the vessel's favor—that is until the coming of steam.

These, of course, were the only natural waterways, but there were the early and later "cuts" made. Canals, which as Mills suggested, had attempted to move the boat traffic inland and have it convert from the slow and unpredictable sail and pole to modern and fast moving steam.

The most modern map shows evidence of this three hundred-year-old boat path, which had obviously been recorded orally for much of this time. What surprised me more, though, was the continuation of that same oral tradition. There were several names being used by the present-day Cape boatman that hadn't appeared in print since 1822, and a good many others that had never appeared printed anywhere, but were still common knowledge.

There are still a few men and women around who could remember the sailing freight boats and the large steamers. There were many more, dozens in fact, who worked on the little gasoline-powered freight boats before the waterway was cut and the highway paved in the 1930s. Besides these, there were the older commercial fishermen who'd put a lifetime in the creek, and all of them carried this oral outline of the waterways. Some were illiterate, but even those who could read had no need for maps.

Papas Creek was still being called "Porpoise" despite a change a hundred years previous. The same was sometimes true of Casino and Cassena, and Five Creeks, the anchorage last recorded for freight boats in 1822 was still Five Creeks. The Horns too had long since gone from the charts and had probably washed away by the 1890s. Still today it was the "Horns." No one I asked had heard of the sand ridges and the guess usually was made that it had some connection to Ramhorn Creek—which might have been true in some sense for there's another Ramhorn—Horns combination to the south of Charleston.

I don't think I came across anyone who'd heard of architect Robert Mills, or had any idea of when the first dredging was done. The cut now marked Clubhouse Creek was still called "The Island Cut," which could lead to Jones Stake. (It's said that this was the artesian well where inn owner Jones watered his marsh-grazing cattle, but the well itself was probably drilled to provide freshwater for steam-powered boats). Since Mills was subcontracting the actual work to the plantation owners living close by, their names have also left behind. Jones Cut came next. And beyond that, the Intracoastal Waterway is still known and printed as Mathews Cut. The industrious Mathews also had a ferry across the Cooper River that's remembered today as the slightly altered Mathis Ferry.

Out toward the beach, the government's century-old designation of Marsh Island had stopped no one from calling Bowman's land "Mill Island." The same maps could call Eagle Hammock, Morants Point, but it remained Eagle Hammock.

Beyond the maps there were, as I said, the dozens of ranges that were still being used, and creeks, coves and points that had never been officially titled could be read off like street names—some ancient, some put there yesterday.

To come in from shrimping at Santee (everything north of Cape Shoals) you ran into the second dip of the Murphy Island woods, then swinging in close to Northeast Point, rounded Cowpen Point, until you see the daylight through Slack Reach. On your left was the shallow water of the Ballast Cove Rock, with the pile of ballast rocks leftover from Scotsman Bowman's windmill adventure. Ahead lay Horsehead tower, Shark Point and the Three Sisters before the Cut carried you home.

There were many more. I say "were," but they haven't changed. Heading down Big Creek (Five Fathom), you pass the tiny cassena shrub called Turkey Bush, the Number Ten, a sagging, unpainted marker, designating a forgotten path of the inland waterway. Heading out across the bay (Bulls) you pass another rounded cassena called The Big Head, which stood at the entrance of Long Creek, which was, for the African American population, once The Psalm presumably because it was the answer to their seafood prayers.

Oysterhouse lies ahead. Most claim this site was once used for the shucking of oysters here in the middle of the bay, but Captain Joe Cumbee remembers it as a storage house that used the rising tides to keep oysters fresh until they could be carried elsewhere for shucking. Anyway an oyster rock remains, but the house has been long gone a good sixty or seventy years.

There are a good many others that have disappeared—many the victims of natural, and man-made filling. Cow Pasture Bay, Terrapin Creek, Seine Bay and The Beach, which once lay at the entrance to McClellanville's Jeremy Creek, are now covered completely by dredge fill. The various small slues, or "docks," that ran off these creeks have all been filled in. Broad Marsh at its head isn't so broad as it once was. The landing there, which we call Galilee, has been renamed the equally Biblical Jericho.

To the south, Shellmore Oyster Company became Cape Romain Lookout subdivisions, and reverted to Shellmore subdivision. The truly ancient salt ponds of the Sewee Indians had been marked by a government refuge tower and the spot is still called Saltpond tower, though the tower has been gone fifteen or more years. To the north, the Palmetto Plantation house was replaced during the Depression with a small, bright-stuccoed house. Some still say Palmetto, but for many it was the Pink House until Hurricane Hugo removed that reminder. The waterway came through here during the 1930s, erased Chandler Island and took out another ancient landmark, Crockamorass Creek. Morass was the French Huguenot term for swamp, which hadn't been on a map since a French edition of 1771, but the DuPre family of Palmetto had hung on to it. These island rice fields were in "the morass" and where these drained into the marsh was the crack of the morass, which became Crackamorass, which, of course, had ended up with the boatmen as "Crackofmyass." That's euphonious for most.

There's poetry here if you know where to look for it, and it's easy enough to refute the claim made by Robert Mills and Washington Irving that somehow an Indian name was more conducive to good poetry and song. Irving complained in particular of the "Mill Creek" in his own Sleepy Hollow—but out "Mill Creek," as commonplace as it sounds, still had a poetic life of its own. I've seen it labeled very early as "Schooner Creek" and in the 1940s, it was referred to as George Mill's Creek, apparently after a market duck hunter famous for shooting fifty-four mallards with one shell (what gauge?). But taken at its true name—just plain Mill Creek—we know we are traveling into the eccentric John Bowman's domain, and that's a journey worthy of Irving.

Bowman, on remittance, from his father the mayor of Glasgow, cut quite a swath along the South Carolina coast. In about 1790 he paid Jonathan Lucas to design and build a rice mill that would revolutionize the planting of rice everywhere. (The Murphy Island marsh would be diked in as a result.) He shot off his brother-in-law's leg in a duel held at the Santee Ferry Landing. He built a wind-driven sawmill in the middle of seemingly nowhere and staked a claim to thousands of acres of surrounding marsh in an attempt to monopolize the wind. That's our Mill Island. That's our Cape Romain. So despite the mundane name of Mill Creek we have a history as strange as any found in Sleepy Hollow.

As for Gene Morrison, the captain, who had introduced me to this wondrous world of names and ranges, I'm sad to report (sad for me—happy for him) that he's given them up all together. Over the years he's converted his shrimp boat to radar, then radar and Loran, and finally, a computerized navigational system that allows his course to be plotted from the moment he leaves from the dock.

He carried me out shrimping last season to show me how it worked. A disc was slipped into the computer, and the wheel responded. If he wanted to personally alter the course, he turned a small knob, positioned just to the right of his chair. The drags for shrimp that we made were marked out in colored lines on the screen, and each of the four drags had its own color.

It was no longer necessary to look for lightning-struck pines and clumps of sea oats. Creeks did not have to be named or even numbered. There were numbers—long sequences of shifting digits on a Loran screen, lazy yellow marks on a computer screen. In fact, as he pointed out, the wheelhouse windows could be painted black, and it would have made no difference.

They are not painted black, however. Son of a Cape boatman, grandson of another, he drinks coffee and idly watches what remains of the square bush close on the big lighthouse. He does watch. But his faith is in the machines, and I can tell that he is as amazed and happy about this current technology as I'd been on that afternoon twenty-seven years before, when he sat me down, and explained that it all had a shape, a name and a meaning.

When Gene Morrison retired, he set up a workshop in his McClellanville back yard and began to produce wooden models of our lighthouses (among other things). He even did a model lighthouse display for Bud Hill's Village Museum, a display that came complete with houses and trees—with ranges in miniature. Next he wrote a memoir called A Fisherman's Life. *When* Message in a Bottle *was made into a movie, Nicholas Sparks called and asked if there was a fisherman Paul Newman could interview in order to get ready for his part. I suggested Gene and mailed out a copy of* A Fisherman's Life. *Paul Newman showed up on Gene's door unannounced and was twenty minutes into the two-day interview, before Gene said, "You're Paul Newman, aren't you?" I hadn't gotten around to telling Gene that the actor might come by, but luckily Gene and his wife Nancy had (when dating) snuck off to Charleston and seen* Cat on a Hot Tin Roof *in 1958, which was why Gene could recognize him now.*

Originally published in *The Low Country Heritage Society Anthology*

Robert Mills's Inland Passage

South Carolina's Robert Mills was the first native-born American trained in architecture and is known to the nation as the designer of the Washington Monument. Closer to home, he is remembered, as well, for the numerous courthouses he built about the state and, of course, as designer of the Historical Society's own Fireproof Building in Charleston. Though these accomplishments are certainly of the first order, Mills left behind another legacy of a different, but no less monumental nature.

Returning home from Baltimore in 1820, the architect was appointed to the Board of Public Works and in this capacity he was for a brief time responsible for South Carolina's ambitious canal program. In order to boost the falling trade at the port of Charleston, the state had begun this work in 1818 and would spend, over the next ten years, the considerable sum of two million dollars in order to obtain two thousand miles of navigable streams. (How the money was spent, why and by whom can be found in *Internal Improvements in South Carolina 1817–1828*, a reprint of "Reports of the Superintendent of Public Works" compiled by David Kohn and privately printed in Washington in 1938.)

This system of course has long since been abandoned, but remnants of it remain. One portion, a portion for which Mills had direct responsibility, was forty miles north of Charleston in the Cape Romain area, and much of his work there has been incorporated into our Intracoastal Waterway. I often traveled it on a daily basis.

Little had been written about this passage before or has been since, but reporting as acting commissioner in 1822, Mills described in some detail the attempts that had been made to speed travel through the fifty miles of creeks, inlets and bays that joined Charleston Harbor to the mouth of the Santee River. Referred to vaguely as "the inland passage," "the Santee path" or "Congaree boat trail," this difficult route twisted its way behind the sometimes shelter of the Sea Island and was shallow for most of its length and dangerously exposed in the Bulls Bay area. It was avoided when possible. Ships could put out to sea at the mouth of the Santee, and further inland at the Santee Canal that had been completed in 1800 in order that cargo coming from upstate could bypass this same section of coast.

Though work on the Cape waterways had begun several years earlier, it appears to have been completed under Mills's administration, and he was certainly the new waterways' most vocal supporter. The actual construction of the canals was done by William Mathews, who, by connecting Awendaw and Brown's Creek and improving the channel with Jones Cut and adding Mathews Cut at present-day McClellanville, made it possible for schooners to bypass much of Bulls Bay.

Mills states that before this, boats attempting to deliver cotton to Charleston were often forced to wait on the Bay's edge at Five Creeks (now Five Fathom Creek) for as long as two weeks in order to gain a favorable breeze. Sometimes growing impatient, they went on and were carried out to sea by the ebb tide. The new route, though far safer, was being ignored however, because "there is an aversion generally with the ignorant to depart out of the beaten tract they have been in the habit of pursuing." (The reluctance of the boatman in this case might be due to the fact that the new canal was only twenty-seven feet wide and five feet deep—perhaps sufficient for the small steamboats he envisioned but not for these sailing "schooners.")

To the north of this section, Mathews had made an additional cut through the end of Jeremy Island, which shortened the passage on to the Santee and then crossed through the delta and headed to reach Georgetown, as well. Working with slaves and oxen these narrow canals would probably have been no more difficult (difficult enough) than the rice field canals of the day, but in connecting the Santee with Winyah Bay, Mills reports that the crews of Thomas Pinckney were with "great labor and perseverance" chopping their way through a forest of cypress. To the south of the Cape were other problems. R.T. Morrison (my great-great-great grandfather) had made cuts at the Sullivan's Island narrows, Price's Inlet and Bull Island, but had failed to block off the bypassed creek beds. Mills chided Morrison in print, pointing out that unless the original creeks were blocked the new cuts would silt in. As can be seen, the general plan behind these cuts was to move the traffic as far as possible from the ocean and as close as possible to the mainland. This would allow planters on the coasts easier access and give the steamboats opportunities to take on fuel and water. With this in mind Mills suggested further cuts through Alligator Creek and Sewee

Bay—routes used over a century later by the Army Corp of Engineers when, on the eve of WWII, they completed the Intracoastal Waterway.

The work of the Corps deserves mention here, for it involves a second and even better known South Carolinian, John C. Calhoun. According to Aubrey Parkman's *History of the Waterways of the Atlantic Coast of the United States* (a Corps publication) it was Secretary of the Treasury Albert Gallatin who in 1808 proposed an Intracoastal Waterway along the Eastern seaboard. But it was Calhoun, who actually tried to pass Gallatin's plan through Congress in 1815, only to have his bill vetoed by James Madison, who agreed with the need but felt it unconstitutional. While serving as secretary of war, in 1819, Calhoun succeeded, stressing the defensive value of such measures, and it was Calhoun who advocated the extensive use of the Army Corps of Engineers to carry out this work.

However, the Corps was given only sporadic support in the years that followed, and not until after the Civil War did nationalistic fervor become strong enough to support federally financed canal projects. Much of our Eastern seaboard Intracoastal Waterway system was completed then, with, as I mentioned, the Cape sections being extensively widened and straightened during the Great Depression. This work sped to completion as the threat of hostile German submarines off our shores became more and more likely.

My old friend, Captain Joe Cumbee, recalls working on the dredge when it cut behind Cape Romain's Jeremy Island in the 1930s. He said the ground was high enough that cows were feeding beside the dredge. And he mentioned the dredges bogging down to the north of Georgetown, because the spent lead shot from countless duck hunters clogged the dredge pipes. He also recalled that as a boy (around 1911) the Mathews Cut section of the waterway was badly silted in, but that the steam tug *Dixie* was still using it to tow lumber to Georgetown. The small gasoline-powered freight boats that were supplying McClellanville used that way on occasion but still crossed the Bay when possible. Waterway traffic in that day was not a cut-and-dried affair, he recalls. When the Corps got a small appropriation, they would make a small improvement. Traveling south of Norfolk, many required guides to find their way through the resulting maze of the creeks and inlets being favored as a route. (Joe didn't mention it but an early waterway guide warns that boaters crossing Bulls Bay should watch for waterway markers being intentionally moved by the citizens of Awendaw. When a misdirected boat ran aground they were charged by the locals for a tow off the bar.)

As for Gallatin and Calhoun's dream to link North with South through trade, the Corps' statistics suggest it remained only a dream. Though the Southern half of the waterway (south of Norfolk) is heavily traveled, the commercial traffic remains "short haul" and it is only recreational vessels that exchange Southern parts for Northern, and vice versa.

Mills too had written of North–South traffic in his statistics, published in 1826, but his grand dream for waterway traffic was actually East–West—a system of waterways that would someday connect Charleston first with Columbia and then with a couple of short stage rides included—go on to the Pacific. (This pamphlet was not reprinted by Kohn but can be found in the Special Collections at the College of Charleston.) The rewards for the state would be great, of course. Commerce would supplement a dangerous reliance on a single-crop economy (rice or cotton) and the sickly swamp regions of the Lowcountry would be drained. Health and prosperity would follow the course of these waterways. (In a related plan that was published in Kohn, Mills proposed that the swamplands of the Lowcountry be bought and drained and resold as valuable farmlands, with the profits to be used to free the slaves and return them to Africa.)

East–West, North–South, despite the best of intentions these plans were being quickly abandoned. Even where geography could be overcome, the growing sectionalism placed insurmountable boundaries about the state's perimeters, while the railroad was making the canals within the state obsolete. Historian D.D. Wallace summed up the canal enterprise as follows, "The pathetic faith as to the possibilities of fleets on rivers that a child could wade for months during the year became a public delusion." Harsh words perhaps, for in Europe such rivers were being used. Still, many of Mills's contemporaries would agree with Wallace. Kohn's reprints are photostats of the original engineer's reports and in the margin of most have been inked in such critical comments as "MORE MONEY" and "Let's have the Bay Boats. Leave the Santee Canal alone."

This criticism, over one hundred fifty years old, has a familiar ring, for it returns us to the original subject of Cape Romain's inland passage. The plans of a progressive-minded Mills, Calhoun and others were not without repercussions, for nature bent out of shape will have her revenge. The builders of the Santee Canal, which would bypass the Cape, determined in the 1790s that there was a considerable difference in elevation between the Cooper and Santee Rivers, and this information, I've read, was used in the 1930s to initiate the rediversion of the Santee River and the construction of the hydro-electric plants of the then-created Lakes Moultrie and Murray. Present-day newspaper accounts complete the story. Though successful as a recreational area, the lakes could not generate the expected power and had to be supplemented by coal-burning generators. The altered Cooper River began dumping the former Santee's unmanageable amounts of silt into Charleston Harbor, and the water of the Santee, first diverted in 1800, is about to be redirected through a multi-million dollar canal. Enough freshwater must be left in the Cooper, however, to supply the needs of the industrial park that has been built there. Meanwhile, the bypassed Cape Romain marshes have been declared a National Wilderness area, which requires a clean air status that could stop further coal-burning industries from being built along the banks of the Cooper. It's a curious entanglement—a lesson of history, which not even the likes of nimble minded Robert Mills could administer to.

Recently, financial support for the continued dredging of the Intracoastal Waterway was drastically cut. Apparently the amount of barge traffic doesn't warrant the expense and the wartime threat from submarines waiting off shore has passed. The waterway here at McClellanville has silted in so badly that instead of having the guaranteed twelve feet, we're reduced to four, and the larger shrimp boats can only cross the waterway and make their way to the ocean during high water. But some funding is on the way.

Originally published in *Carologue*

Mystery at Saltpond

In the late 1600s a group of large outfitted canoes, bearing some of the last Sewee Indians, headed into the Atlantic. Cheated by unscrupulous Indian traders and convinced that England could not be far over the horizon, they had decided to cut out the middlemen and go there themselves. The trip was a disaster. The few to survive the first storm were taken up by pirates and sold into slavery in the Caribbean.

Despite the Sewee's dubious distinction of being the only Indian tribe to attempt a trans-Atlantic voyage, English explorer John Lawson wrote in 1700 of his great respect for the remaining tribe members he found occupying the area between the Cooper and Santee Rivers. He was particularly impressed with the way they lived in relation to the land. This use of resources is what interested me when I was studying the Cape Romain area, attempting to determine how humans had survived over the centuries. Hence the Sewee clam middens at Awendaw were difficult to ignore, and I zeroed in on those at the U.S. forest site of Saltpond.

A midden is basically a garbage pile. It's a collection of kitchen debris and there at Saltpond, large quantities of shell are mixed with scraps of pottery, conch tools and bits of stone and bone. The pottery is distinctively Sewee and the middens had been officially dated to AD 1600, plus or minus one hundred years. Strung out along the Intracoastal Waterway, there were four in all, and though badly bruised by the twentieth century, all, when I first found them, were roughly the same size—about thirty-five feet wide and one hundred twenty feet long. (Incidentally, they're protected by federal law so you can't collect artifacts.)

Shell middens are common. They're found throughout the Lowcountry and throughout the world. These at Saltpond, however, had one slight distinction: no oyster shells. They consist only of clamshells and a few snails and conchs. Still, this hardly makes them unique. Numerous explanations occurred, the most obvious being that clams were the main food source. Yet mixed middens are close by. More importantly, beneath the humus surrounding the clam middens is an extensive layer of mixed shell. I wasn't the first to notice this. At least one professional archeologist had labeled them "puzzling" and several local residents had remarked on the missing oyster shells.

The clue, as I saw it, was in the observation made by Lawson in 1700. He was amazed by the economy of effort with which these people lived. Why, then, had the Sewee gone to the trouble to segregate and pile up hundreds of bushels of clamshells?

I can't claim any particularly scientific method to my inquiry. I simply assumed from the very beginning that I was looking at architecture and so most likely this separation of shells had a religious significance. What added to this conviction—made it a certainty—was the close proximity of the Sewee shell ring. That ring was certainly architecture.

First appearing along the south Georgia coast about four thousand years ago, shell rings are the oldest example of architecture in North America. They vary greatly in size and location. Today some are surrounded by marsh, others by dense woods. Though a variety of food debris is found in them, they are composed chiefly of oyster shells. They were also found to contain the earliest examples of pottery in North America. The discovery of similar but slightly earlier rings in Colombia, South America, caused several theories of South American colonization to be formulated—none strongly supported. Little else is known of the rings' origin or purpose, but it is surmised that the builders lived on the perimeter in flimsy shelters. Since the centers of the rings were found to be relatively clean, there is a strong possibility they served a religious purpose. Archeologists do tend to agree that the presence of pottery and circular construction meant that a sedentary village life had come to a previously nomadic people. We are seeing the rudiments of modern civilization.

What did this have to do with the Sewee? Nothing, and yet a great deal. The Sewee shell ring is the northernmost of the remaining rings. The massive ring is about two hundred feet across and has an eighty-foot interior. The highest point at the northeastern edge is fourteen feet, but the opposite side is gone, leaving not a ring but a C-shaped enclosure. Built in 1200 BC, the Sewee ring is the youngest—but the Sewee didn't build it. They didn't arrive here for at least another twenty-four hundred years. Still there seems to be a connection. The ring is located in a marsh slough just in from the Sewee clam middens and twenty years earlier a state archeology project had come up with some curious data that might link the sites together.

In one portion of the ring, water-worn pottery was mixed with the shell several feet above any previously known tide level. This suggested to me that for some reason the shells had been rearranged at a later date. Finally, and most importantly, beginning on the eastern rim of the early ring of predominately oyster shells was a narrow apron of clamshells that lead to a small man-made peninsula in the cove. Somebody had obviously built something and the question was "What?"

Ah, the pursuit of knowledge. I quit work and began to visit the site regularly—sometimes just sitting for hours turning a conch hammer over in my hand. I read nothing but French anthropologists. Though we generally think of totems in terms of the familiar bear, buffalo or eagle, anthropologist Levy-Bruhl described the totem significance of animals and edible plants: "These are, or may become, protectors and benefactors to the group as a whole." There was nothing here to disqualify a reverence for clams, no matter how silly that might sound to modern man. Though harder to get through, Levi-Strauss was saying the same.

The clamshells as building material could have a religious significance, but where was this leading? By now I was sleeping only a few hours a night, obsessed with the question of "What?" And then at 4:30 one February morning the obvious suddenly became very obvious, I'd been walking around in the midst of a giant calendar.

If I were to stand in the middle of the shell ring and face due east, I would be looking along the axis of the best preserved and southernmost of the Sewee clam middens. I went to sleep immediately. The next morning I went back to work—back to a normal life. And I waited.

On the morning of the spring equinox (March 21) I stood in the ring and watched the sun rise exactly over the crest of the southernmost clam midden. That was simple. But the ring was now separated from the other three middens by a thick forest. I hired a surveyor to pinpoint the exact locations of the other middens and then extended poles into the marsh to establish a sight line—a line that would lead back to the ring. The survey proved that the middens all "pointed" in toward the ring's center.

On the day of the summer solstice (June 21) the sun rose along the axis of the northernmost midden. This is the first day of summer, the longest day of the year, and marks the northernmost position that the sun will rise. From now on the sunrise would move back south, back toward the first or equinox midden. That left only the two center middens to account for. Using marine navigation tables, a friend gave me two approximate target dates. Twenty days later, on July 11, I watched the sun rise over the first of the center middens.

I'd started this project with an almost total ignorance of Indian calendars. They were rare east of the Mississippi, I soon learned, but common in the American West and even more plentiful in Central America where a few calendar priests still live. In these places, the topic is popular enough to have become a distinct archeological discipline. And not long after that last mentioned observation, I discovered that the Mayan month was twenty days, a measurement adopted throughout Central America. I had a calendar sunrise at twenty days. This should have been encouraging news but it wasn't.

There are no references to these months, called "uninals," north of the Rio Grande River. The clam middens at Saltpond were eroded. The surveyor had guessed at a center. Perhaps it was a "lucky" guess. The evidence for the equinox and summer solstice seemed solid—irrefutable. But this last reading of twenty days I put down to coincidence.

Twenty days later, on August 11, the sun rose over the crest of the remaining midden. Though the middens were not equal distances apart, the increasing speed with which the sunrise moved along the horizon as it approached the equinox caused the two center middens to be equidistant, in time. If the "equal time" was a coincidence it was a double one. And the strangest revelation was to come a week later in the library.

In the late 1970s Anthony Aveni and a team of archeologists studying the Mayan Temple of Venus in Copan, Honduras, had drawn base lines between the temple and stone pillars set in the distant hillsides. They had come up with a division of time that was the mirror image of the one at Saltpond. (Neither calendar marks the winter solstice, so half the year remains an unbroken blank.) Aveni couldn't explain all his observations but he was certain the Copan calendar had an agricultural application. At least one reading related to the agricultural year by announcing the beginning of the rainy season. (Today, people living near Copan still plant by that schedule.)

Of course, what applied to tropical growing seasons wouldn't apply directly here, but the idea of an agricultural calendar did. The Sewee wintered slightly inland, but for the rest of the year they came to the marsh to gather shellfish and plant corn.

Though few solar calendars were found on this side of the Mississippi, there were several references to solstice and equinox observations, and these were often tied to planting schedules. The date for first corn planting might come in accordance with the moon, but it was related first to the spring equinox. In Copan the concern was with rain. In Awendaw the problem was frost. (To avoid the cold, the present inhabitants still plant their corn in the middle of March.)

It's possible that marking the summer solstice had an equally dramatic implication. All over the Southeast the green husk was celebrated. This was the day on which the first of the corn crop could be eaten. To eat it sooner might mean death to the violator for this was a sacred time of purging and renewal. And though the celebration date varied with the growing season, the corn here at Saltpond matured in time for the solstice to be its mark.

For the remaining two middens (the inner ones) I could only guess at a purpose. At least two corn crops and sometimes three were planted by the Indians and these middens could have marked dates for planting. Numerous celebrations are mentioned, their relation to these two middens is probably unknowable.

Other mysteries remained on the site. One small collection of clamshells on the edge of the marsh slough lays on a sight line indicating it was probably the position of an intermediate post—something common to other known calendars. The clamshell apron and accompanying peninsula leading away from the shell ring, however, remain unexplained.

Some loose ends. The sun, it seems, was the principal deity throughout the Southeast. And there was nothing in the studies of the anthropologists I first read to suggest that totems hadn't been involved in the calendar construction. In that simpler (and more complicated) time the heavens and earth and the mundane and spiritual were closely intertwined. At Saltpond, the relationship will no doubt remain a mystery, for the particulars of the Sewee cosmology were buried with the tribe.

Why was this South Carolina calendar so similar to the one built centuries earlier and thousands of miles away in Honduras? I recall an article that suggest on the basis of pottery the Sewee were remnants of a mound-building tribe pushed eastward to this coastal area centuries earlier. Such a tribe would have been part of the greater Mississippian culture and therefore would have had trading contacts with the Aztecs, the diffusers of Mayan culture. That also was too slender a thread to hang an answer on, so I was content to let the similarities remain a mystery. On the whole, I was satisfied with my Saltpond calendar just as it was.

No one in a position of authority was convinced with my findings. I don't think any state or federal agency I sent my information to bothered to send someone to look at the site. I don't think they even read the paper all the way through or at all. But that was all right, for it allowed my friends and me to go unaccompanied on the appointed mornings and watch the sun rise across the middens.

In the years since my discovery, the marks and stakes have gradually disappeared and then the two northernmost middens began to disappear, as well. The wakes of boat traffic in the Intracoastal Waterway reached them even before September of 1989. That's when Hurricane Hugo hit the site dead center and crushed the encircling forest of mature loblolly pines, hickories and oaks, leaving behind a broken, snarled and impassable landscape.

And now for a footnote. Every valid history requires at least one. Remember the story of the Sewee voyage to England? The rest is just supposing. It's known that the ship *Carolina*, bearing the first permanent English colonists, made landfall at Cape Romain and sailed into Bulls Bay on March 17, 1670. The channel they took lies directly off the Sewee ring and the southernmost midden. Though a twenty-foot embankment of dredge fill has now altered the view, at that time the ship would have been seen entering the Bay. And they had sailed into the Sewee's horizon at an auspicious time of year.

Governor Sayles and the others on board were happily surprised by the welcome the Indians extended. Lifted to the shoulders of the excited natives, the Englishmen were carried to the "ye Hutt Palace" and treated with "chearfull entertainment." On March 20, only one day before the spring equinox, they sailed off toward the Port Royal vicinity where they found no welcome at all. They settled instead in Charleston and the Sewee were soon helping to protect and feed them, and eventually became slavers on their behalf. The Indians' reward for this service was not what they had expected.

For many tribes the sun, which was a god itself, rose in the east from a mythical land of bounty. How much truer that must have seemed to the sun-worshipping Sewee when, in 1670 they saw the English ship enter in the same place as their rising sun.

When the English traders cheated them, how simple it must have seemed to sail eastward in their great canoes—sail eastward into the rising sun. They couldn't know what we take for granted; the sun is but a rising star.

All this happened twenty years ago. I was forty. Perhaps it was my mid-life crisis. I spent six months on the project, an all-consuming six months, and like to think I was profoundly altered, for in the hours spent in the quiet of that shell ring spinning those conch tools in my hands, I was able to form at least a notion of "a sheltering sky." At one point I even enjoyed a momentary vision of a grand spherical shape arching above the site, arching above me as a clear but protective shell. Perhaps this image was unconsciously borrowed from some library book diagram I'd come across, but still the experience was a vivid one. "The Universe appears to be on the side of love." That's what Reverend Cook, the Presbyterian minister, said at a wedding the other day. I hope he's right. If not, at least, it's on the side of beauty.

As for my theory, I still think I'm right. Actually you can just look at an aerial photo of the area (the earlier the better) and see all the elements of the calendar. If I'd known what I was looking at, I could have figured the site out from home. As for the response of the Forest Service and the State Archeology Department: In those dealings I learned something about bureaucracy and about myself, as well. Back in the mid '60s the state of South Carolina, with Forest Service's, help had done an ambitious dig on this site and in print announced the Sewee ring was a large fish trap. The fact that their fish trap was above high water and had been much higher above high water when it was built could be explained by dismissing all scientific evidence to the contrary and saying that the ocean along the entire Eastern seaboard was once much higher than we thought. This was ridiculous but I suspect laughing at that notion at the beginning of my own paper (the first version) made me no friends among the bureaucrats and I lacked the patience to make amends. A bureaucracy is a strange animal with its own private habits and dispositions, a strange land where entrenchment and a non-disruptive laziness can often make for a successful career. "How other people do life" is far more complicated than any calendar theory I could come up with.

As the innermost tip of the northernmost clam midden was washing into the Intracoastal Waterway, the departing humus revealed a surface of the midden covered over in uniform clam shells, all laid with their backs facing up, and these were edged with a distinctive outline of small conch shells which tapered off in the direction of the Sewee ring. Stuart Mackintosh, a local Indian buff, told me that a few feet inland from where I stood there had once been three circles of shell, each about three feet across—one was of conchs, one of clams and one of snails. He said pot hunters had dug those up thirty years before. Now erosion has taken the entire midden. It all passes. I'll let that be the lesson.

Originally published in *charleston* magazine

Carolina Light

Anxious moments. Eyes strain at the salt-laced blackness. Prayers are muttered and maybe curses cursed, until finally, "There! There it is! There!"

Even today, in this age of satellite tracking and radar, few sights are more welcome to the mariner than the reassuring beam of a lighthouse. It's a guarantee of sorts. The timing of the flash gives that light's identity and dictates a course to set. And with the coming of day, the distinctive painted pattern creates a "day marker" that does the same. Yes, we know them well, even the most landlocked of us. The "guiding light" has found its way onto the front of everything from soap operas to religious pamphlets—a symbol of both constancy and safe haven.

And at a time when shipping is turning to electronic aids, and many lighthouses have been decommissioned and some threatened with destruction, interest in the towers themselves is reviving. A nationwide Lighthouse Preservation Society has been formed to aid in their restoration, and Congress has allocated funds to help. They've become a favorite of artists. South Carolina has even designated that all eight of our lighthouses will eventually appear on the state's duck stamps, and other states are honoring their own lights. Fans subscribe to lighthouse magazines and travel the coast to see them all.

No doubt lighthouses or at least signal lights go back far earlier, but the first recorded structure was built for the harbor at Alexandria, Egypt, in 3000 BC. This light of the Pharaoh burned for a thousand years, and the Romans are known to have kept lights, as well, but it wasn't until the expanding of commerce in the Middle Ages that Europe was to see a revival of light towers. The Italians were probably the first and had a tower built in Genoa in 1161. Christopher Columbus's uncle was tending that one three hundred years later.

The first lighthouse in America was built in Boston in 1716, and the cooperative nature of those Northern climes did seem to lend itself better to such enterprises. But the Morris Island lighthouse, put at the mouth of Charleston Harbor in 1768, was only the nation's seventh.

Towers of wood were often used, but brick and steel seemed the most durable for South Carolina. A height of a hundred feet or better allowed a good light to shine about eighteen miles or a bit beyond, and with a flat, featureless coastline a daylight mark was welcome as well. Records are scant, but it's assumed most of the early ones were slave-built and considering the isolation and logistics involved, monumental accomplishments. The lamp or light that rested in the top was usually framed of iron, steel and brass and surrounded with glass. Inside would be found a flame of some sort. Coal was an early fuel. So was pitch. Candles were also in use and then lamps burning first sperm whale oil, then mineral oil and finally kerosene that could be burned under pressure much like today's Coleman lantern. Electricity came last and in these isolated sites was provided by generators and batteries.

To magnify the flame, reflectors were placed behind it, but the real revolution came when the lens, most specifically the French Fresnel lens, went into use. A complex combination of prisms set into concentric circles, this lens succeeded in concentrating the light to a powerful beam. With the establishment of a Light House Board in 1852, a systematic supervision of light keepers and a major overhaul of lights occurred. As our state's records show, towers were built higher or replaced, and Fresnel lenses went on the major lights.

A typical day for the light keeper revolved around maintaining a neat and orderly light and grounds. Working in shifts, a keeper and his assistant and often a mechanic would clean and polish the lenses, haul oil up the hundred or so stairs, reset the "clock" weights that caused the lamp to turn and prepare for the coming of light—when their duty was to maintain the flame. Located as they were on isolated Sea Islands, it's not surprising that complaints of loneliness and monotony were common.

In 1768 by order of the English king, the Morris Island light, a simple octagonal tower, was erected to mark the main channel into Charleston's harbor. The "ingenious architect" responsible was Samuel Crody, who also finished up St. Michael's church. In 1857 this light was extensively repaired and then in 1861, because it was the property of the U.S. government, the Morris Island lighthouse entered into a dispute that was enlarged to include

Fort Sumter and further enlarged to become the Civil War. At this point Confederate forces destroyed the light, tower and all, and the island became a blood-soaked battleground. The Union would eventually replace the light with an anchored lightship (the crew of which reported picking up barrelsful of human skulls from the beach and burying them inland) and with a second range light mounted on the roof of a Sullivan's Island house.

In 1876 a new light was begun. Called the Charleston Main Light, it required a foundation of 264 pilings driven into the sand and capped with another eighteen inches of timber and five feet of concrete. On top of this rose a 180-foot brick tower boasting a Fresnel lens of the first order. To accommodate the keepers, three substantial houses of Victorian design were added near the base as well as a dozen smaller buildings—everything provided, from a one-room schoolhouse to a chicken coop. Gardens were tended and considerable livestock kept. Visitors came out from the city to fish, hunt wild pigs and relax and enjoy the breezes, thus creating a fondly remembered community life.

In 1938 the Coast Guard took over administration of the lighthouses, and the Morris Island lighthouse was electrified and permanent keepers removed. Since then another sixteen hundred feet of the island has washed away. In 1962 the light was abandoned, and today at high tide ocean waves surround the structure perched on its pilings.

The light taking its place signals from nearby Sullivan's Island. Triangular in shape and 163 feet tall, this experimental metal design boasts the only lighthouse elevator in America. When lit in 1962 it was also the brightest light in the Western Hemisphere, visible twenty-six miles at sea. The original lamp burned with twenty-eight million candlepower, a dangerous level and the power was lowered considerably the following year. At the base are several handsome Victorian buildings of the Life Saving Station—a curious juxtaposition, especially when you consider that this ultramodern lighthouse will probably be the last built in our country.

Sixty miles to the north, the Georgetown lighthouse is actually the oldest surving light in the state. In 1789 a "gratious cession" of North Island land was provided and a decade later construction began. The light was lit in 1801. Built of wood, this seventy-two-foot tower was destroyed in a storm in 1806 and replaced in 1812. Massive brick with stone supports and steps, this replacement took some punishment when the Confederate forces put it out of commission, but the Union made repairs following the Civil War. Probably the most dramatic event involving the light or at least its surroundings was the great hurricane that wiped out North Island's summer village. Whole houses with occupants inside and lamps still burning drifted out to sea.

The last of South Carolina's lights to be manned, this one had families in attendance until a 1968 fire destroyed the two main buildings. With families or as bachelors, the light keeper's happiest memories usually revolved around the island's hunting and fishing, which ended for all in 1988 when a fully automated beacon went in.

The next light to be built was just to the south on Cape Romain in 1827. An abandoned windmill on the Cape was being mistaken for the Morris Island lighthouse, a particularly dangerous situation because of the area's extensive shoal. A plan was proposed to place a lighthouse atop the windmill tower, but since no high ground existed for keeper's cabins, a new 654-foot brick tower was built on the next island over. That served until 1857 when a second octagonal tower of 161 feet went into service with a first-class Fresnel lens. Incidentally, this "new" tower leaned considerably. Tradition claims it was built crooked to start with, but the deviation of 3 feet, 8 inches beyond vertical doesn't appear in the records until the 1870s.

Bloodstains are said to have marked the floor of one of the houses, for a keeper reportedly murdered his wife when she received a package of jewels in the mail. A jury set him free, so he went elsewhere and made a bad end. (A Reconstruction incident, a time when allegiance to the United States sometimes took precedence over other virtues. Just joking. Sort of.)

The Cape Romain lighthouse was a favorite destination for beach outings from the mainland, especially for young people intent on courting. Hepburn Morrison served as an assistant here at the turn of the century and declared the "girls loved his uniform." Wearing it, he would stand on his head on the very top of the light and balance there by wrapping his feet around the lightning rod tip. "Just showing off for the ladies," says his granddaughter, Judy Fortner.

Fred Wichman, a Charleston businessman, was born on the lighthouse island and recalled his lighthouse keeper father in a slightly more decorous light. Though a small man and unable to swim, August Wichmann single-handedly rescued the captain of a foundering vessel and then led the exhausted crew the four miles back to the light. On another occasion (at the Hunting Island lighthouse) he attended the light straight through for several days, a devotion to duty that temporarily cost him his eyesight. Also he was partially deaf. Though lightning striking the towers would follow the lightning rod to the ground, the noise inside the structure was quite literally deafening.

In 1937 Cape Romain's tower was electrified and in 1947 shut down completely. As a small boy, restoration contractor Tom Graham was carried down to the marsh edge by his father to see the final shining of this beacon and forty years later volunteered to supervise the weatherizing of both old lighthouses. Funds from the federal government and the cooperation of the U.S. Fish and Wildlife Service have allowed the building to be painted and the vandalized lamp house has been enclosed in glass.

To aid navigation between Charleston and Savannah a light was placed on Hunting Island in 1859. Just three years later Confederate forces reduced this structure to "a mass of brick and rubbish about forty feet high." In 1874 work began on a new ninety-five-foot tower, one built of brick-lined, interchangeable cast-iron sections that could be dismantled and moved if necessary. This was a controversial notion at the time, but only fifteen years later the ocean had encroached to the point where the light and its three accompanying houses had to be disassembled and moved inland about a mile.

Because of malaria fever, St. Helena wasn't considered a good duty spot for keepers—not the only danger, apparently. Captain Wichmann once killed an alligator that approached his wife while she was hanging out clothes.

Long since stopped, the lighthouse now serves as the centerpiece of Hunting Island State Park—and this lighthouse is by far the easiest to visit and enjoy. An automobile ride across causeways and bridges and through a beautiful semi-tropical island takes the place of the earlier ferry trip and tram rail crossing. You can climb the lighthouse's 181 iron steps, which quickly seem like 1,081, and enjoy a fine view of the park's pristine beach and bordering ocean.

In about 1874 another light was being erected at the mouth of the Savannah River on Daufuski Island. Called the Haig Point lighthouse, technically this is not a lighthouse but one of two range lights for the Savannah Harbor. The light was decommissioned in 1924 and is now in the hands of developers.

Local historian Billie Burn describes the two-story house with light tower attached as being "built of virgin timber without a single knothole." She happily recalls how ex-keeper Arthur A. Burn (Pappy) bought the building in 1926 and entered an adventurous retirement. With wife and family as company he fished and shrimped to his heart's content. "He loved this island so much he stated he would not give a teaspoon of Daufuski for the whole of S.C."

In 1890 a ninety-two-foot steel light tower was placed on Hilton Head to work in conjunction with a much shorter range light placed on the beach a mile away. Though perhaps the least impressive architecturally this light does boast the best ghost story. During the ferocious hurricane of 1898 the widowed keeper Adam Fripp was tending the light with his twenty year-old daughter, Caroline. A gust of wind blew out the lamp, and at the same moment Adam was felled by a heart attack. But before dying he urged his daughter to relight and maintain the flame, which she did alone for several more nights. Unfortunately, she never recovered from this ordeal and died three weeks later.

Her ghost, a woman in a gauzy dress, continued to haunt the lighthouse, and when the accompanying keepers' houses were moved to nearby Harbor Town, a glowing blue light would sometimes appear to even the most skeptical viewers. With restoration of these buildings, she abandoned the premises, which are now a deli and a real estate office.

Ironically the newest of South Carolina lights is also the best known. Completed in 1970, this ninety-four-foot tower is built of steel pipe and plywood and painted in bright bands of red and white. It's privately owned, the first such light in America since 1817, and is used by waterway traffic in the area of Hilton Head's Harbor Town.

"Some thought it senseless," reads the sign at the bottom, "to build such a structure and call it 'Fraser's Folly.'" But Fraser, the developer of Hilton Head's Sea Pines resort, had visited seaside communities worldwide and was certain that a lighthouse was needed and that such a lighthouse would have great symbolic impact. He was right. Strategically placed, the harbor-edge structure is also in close proximity to the eighteenth hole of the Harbor Town golf course, and so viewers of the Heritage Golf Classic (and there are many, many millions) have made the Harbor Town lighthouse the state's most recognized landmark, which is perhaps as it should be. A plaque on the tower denotes the first golf club in the New World begun on the greens of South Carolina in 1786.

The pleasures of the original lighthouse keepers were a bit different. Greens were usually reserved for grazing sheep and cattle. While monotony might have been a common complaint on these sometimes lonely sites, most recall them as places of peace and plenty. Lighthouse keeper's son Ludwig Munn tells of a self-sufficiency that was envied on the main land. Ducks by the hundreds flew into the light on stormy nights and were collected in wheelbarrows. Every bed on the island had a duck feather mattress. "There was different kind of fish hawk around back then," he declares. "Bigger. And we'd watch it swooping then set the net. We just took the best of the fish and let the rest go. We salted them and placed them on the roofs to dry."

And of course there was fishing for sport. The Bulls Island lighthouse has long since washed away, but Inga Swendsen Harper, the daughter of another keeper, recalls her daddy catching a channel bass as big as himself. It's said he fished with a hemp line and treble hook the size of a small grappling iron, and when a fish struck he'd throw the rope over his shoulder and run straight up the beach.

Her daddy was from Norway and had been captain of a four-masted schooner. She thought he missed the sea because when his day's work was done he would sit high on the tower steps and gaze at the ocean. And when a good breeze was blowing he'd walk back and forth on the "perch" facing the ocean and sing:

There's moonlight on the sea
There's moonlight on the sea
The night is coming on
And there's moonlight on the sea.

We'll let Inga, the lighthouse keeper's daughter, have the final world here. She wrote this of her life as a small girl on the turn-of-the-century Bulls Island:

> *I remember how I loved to walk on the beach alone. I would gather shells. I have never found such lovely shells anywhere else as those I gathered as a child. When I had walked until I was tired, I would stop by a long log that was just above the high water mark, lying in the sand. The sun and the wind and the tide had bleached it until it looked like silver. I would lie down in the white sand next to the log and watch the sky and the ocean. Usually there were many white clouds in the sky and I would pretend that I could see horses and chariots flying through the sky, or a beautiful castle high up on a mountain, and all kinds of birds and animals. It was wonderful just to lie there and rest and pretend.*
>
> *Then I would watch the ocean, and this was real. I would watch the porpoises chase each other and sometimes they would leap almost completely out of the water, with the sun shining on their slick bodies. I loved the porpoises.*
>
> *We used to hunt for Captain Kidd's treasure. We would all dig, sometimes on the beach, sometimes in the woods. It was there! All we had to do was find it and be rich. Sometimes when digging, we'd hit something hard like metal and the boys would go wild and dig harder and faster. It was only a piece of metal or some lumber from an old wreck. Oh, well! Better luck next time.*
>
> *I remember how each of us would try to be the one to find the first yellow jessamine bloom in the spring, so we could take it to Mama. She loved its fragrance.*
>
> *I remember one night there was a terrible storm and some time before morning Papa heard a noise from down under the house and went to investigate. It was Captain Hepburn Morrison,* [Yes, that's the same young assistant who impressed the girls by standing on his head atop the Cape Romain light.] *our dear Miss Lizzie's brother, and a colored man. They did not have a stitch of clothes on and were shivering in the cold. They did not want to come upstairs and knock at the door for fear Mama would come to the door. They had been out in Mr. Hepburn's sailboat and had been wrecked in the storm. They finally made it to our beach and lay down in the sand until they were able to walk to the lighthouse. Papa wrapped them up in a blanket, brought them upstairs to the fire and made hot coffee for them. They said they had been guided to the shore during the storm by the light from the lighthouse.*

Some somber facts. Actually, Hepburn Morrison came ashore alone. The colored man had drowned during the night, and Hepburn had clung to the corpse (they were on opposite sides of the overturned boat) until daylight and then made it ashore as she describes. Elsewhere in the memoir, Mrs. Harper makes a similar and perhaps intentional mistake by referring to her own father's death from an illness. An old newspaper article mentioned that he died on Bulls Island after a fall. I assume the fall was connected to the Bulls Island lighthouse tower.

Originally published in *South Carolina Wildlife* magazine

Deer and Ticks and Mice on Bulls Island:

My Father William P. Baldwin Jr.

Bulls Island was added to the Cape Roman National Wildlife Refuge in 1935. My father, William P. Baldwin Jr., came to the island in 1938 as the junior refuge manager, but he was actually working as a wildlife biologist. Mr. Dominick and the owners before him had brought cattle, sheep and hogs onto Bulls Island, but they were gone by 1938. One purpose of the refuge was to act as a source of game animals for other sections of the country. My father was to help in this shifting, especially the shifting of turkeys and deer.

As you'll see, my father often took a jaundiced view of his government days in "wildlife management," but his first years at Bulls Island were quite productive. He inventoried everything around him. The work he and his assistant Johnny Lofton did with the loggerhead turtles is still referred to today. And one of the old timers on the island said he saw my father shoot two running deer with a single shot twelve gauge. That was daylight hunting.

I lifted what follows from tape recordings made in 1985.

By trapping I was supposed to reduce the deer herd to within the range's carrying capacity, but we soon discovered that in a maritime forest there was so much green food and acorns it was impossible to entice the deer into the traps. So they decided to shoot the deer and it wouldn't be done by opening to the public the way it's done today. They were afraid of public reaction to public hunting on a refuge. The refuge personnel were to shoot the deer. I was one of two. We tried to day hunt but that was too slow so we decided on shining the deer at night. We had to get a special permit from the South Carolina Game Department, which was shocked but finally came around. We'd walk practically all night long with a headlight shooting deer. On a good night we'd shoot one or two, sometimes three or four. One temporary patrolman worked at this and I worked at it. That winter I personally killed thirty-one deer night hunting. It got so I'd wake up at night—what little sleep was left in a night—with eyes shining at me. I had nightmares of deer eyes shining. I developed a real phobia and finally refused to do it anymore.

Totally illogical to be hunting that way on a refuge, it should be open to the public. Of course we didn't throw the deer away. We skinned them and sold the hides for the benefit of the government. We'd take the dressed deer and give them away to charities and the like in Charleston. The army detachment on Sullivan's Island got a lot of venison.

And of course we studied the deer we shot. We took measurements and examined them for parasites. The ticks were a terrible problem. They affected the deer, the turkeys, the fox squirrels, the human visitors. We were covered with ticks at the end of the day and had to take special precautions with our clothing, keep everything tucked in. We got so we could actually look through binoculars and tell how old a deer was. In examining the carcasses we saw that the old bucks and does would have their ears eaten about a third off—like you'd snipped them off with a pair of scissors. Ticks eating on the ear tips had nibbled them away.

We caught a few fawns in the summer that were so weak they couldn't run. They had so many thousands of ticks gorging on them that they died from loss of blood. Knowing of this extreme population the government sent a Dr. Smith to the island. One of the world's leading tick experts, he stayed in a spare cottage with a crew of six fellows. They were working with the army in anticipation of the coming war. They knew the soldiers would be fighting in countries that would have all sorts of parasites. So every day these six would put on a new batch of clothing that had been dipped in various poisons or at least chemical repellants. The six would start through the woods and at stated intervals they'd stop and pick the ticks off their clothing and record them as to number and species, etc. Frequently you'd see one of these fellows start down the road and they couldn't stand the clothing—it was burning their skin so they'd let out a yell and rip off their clothes. All these were new chemicals, developed in the hope the GI's in the South Pacific could lie around in the bushes with impunity. And eventually they did succeed. I'm sure some of the tick repellants on the market today are a result of those tests—Ticks Off probably is.

A curious thing about those six—one fellow was always the control so he wore untreated clothing. You had to compare to the unprotected. But there was one man of Mediterranean decent. He had olive skin and there was some secretion from his body that repelled the ticks better than anything they had. When he was control it screwed up the records completely. It took them two weeks to figure this out. Then they started over. They made him cook. He stayed behind after that.

In the course of my biological studies I ran trap lines for all kind of rodents. I made study skins that went to the Charleston Museum and the National Museum. I sent up raccoons and the rest. We also collected the ticks from all these, as well, and soon learned what others were learning. The rodents carried the larval stage of the ticks and then raccoon and deer carried the middle stage and the adults. Ticks molt through these three stages and they need a meal of blood to molt and to lay eggs successfully. Through my collections Dr. Smith determined that the island had five species of ticks. If I can remember the names. [*He gives the Latin names for all five and the common names for the three I'm mentioning.*] The dog tick, of course. But the most abundant was the Lone Star tick. The female has a white dot on her back. A related species wasn't as abundant. In the winter we had two small black ticks that the natives called "the winter ticks."

Most people think a tick is a tick but we had five and they all carried diseases in various ways. We know now that the Lone Star is as good a carrier of the Rocky Mountain Spotted Fever as the Dog Tick is.

The missing animals? Of course, Bulls Island wasn't a perfect laboratory. Mr. Dominick had brought in all sorts of livestock—usually the "biggest" of whatever it was. He'd introduced these odd-shaped—stumpy—half-wild, half-domesticated "wild turkeys." One of my first jobs was getting those off the island. We knew that once Bulls Island had had a very large population of opossums and the previous owner had them removed. He wanted to get rid of as many varmints as he could so he had the carcasses of cattle poisoned and apparently the opossums were eliminated completely. But that was before my time. It was an odd mixture and still is. There are no copperhead snakes on the island. No cottontail rabbits. No gray squirrels. We were told that Dominick's stable boy introduced the fox squirrels—he brought a pair as pets. I never saw a fox on the island. The most abundant rodent was the rice rat that lives in damp locations. Well, Bulls Island is nothing but dune ridges with troughs between, so in a wet winter the woods are about 50 percent water and the vegetation, especially at the pond edges, was ideal for rice rats. I don't recall that we ever trapped a cotton rat though. And there were several other rats we didn't find. But interestingly, I trapped a house mouse, which had become naturalized—lived in the wilds. But I only found it in the outer dunes. And curiously enough, each of these house mice had a tiny streak of white on the top of their heads. I thought it was unusual but never wrote any article about it. A few years back I read a scientific article by an investigator who'd trapped house mice in the Florida outer dunes and they were marked with a white streak on the top of the head. Just shows you the marvels of science.

I guess that's about it for today. No. Let me tell you one more story about deer. When I was trying to trap deer we built a couple of corrals and planted them in winter wheat. Nice green food. As I recall I took fine copper wire out of old electric coils. I used it for trip wires, arranged it so that when the deer walked forty feet into the corral they would hit the wire with their foot and pull a release that dropped the entry door. I got to where I could trap a few that way. Now I was living in the Dominick house with Mr. and Mrs. Mills. They took in boarders, mostly birders. Two that were studying birds were Allan Crookshank and his wife, who was also quite a photographer. Her name slips me at the moment. They stayed for several weeks. Allan was a terrific photographer, worked all day in blinds, took a tremendous series of black and white photographs of all kind of wildlife.

Well, this is what happened the first time I'd successfully trapped deer in the corral. I was there in the dark and knew I had several in the corral. I went off to bed and the next morning at breakfast I mentioned to the Crookshanks that I was going out to the corral to take some deer out. I would be putting them in a shipping crate to send them off the island. Of course, he and his wife wanted to photograph the procedure. So they came along. Except I'd never taken deer out of the corral before. That was my mistake. I had the collecting chute all ready and the crate behind it all ready. Mrs. Crookshank got on top of the wooden chute so she could look out on the corral and I was up there as well. Mr. Crookshank was on the ground standing beside the chute. Three deer were inside. A big buck, a doe and a yearling—really just a fawn. It was about nine in the morning. The deer got a good look at us. And the buck ran straight across the corral and jumped. He lowered his antlers and went clear through the heavy wire fence and kept going. The doe panicked, ran in the opposite direction, hit the fence and broke her neck. She dropped dead. And the yearling trotted around the inside of the fence and entered the collecting chute. And I pulled the release cord. But the yearling had changed it's mind and turned around midway. The door hit it in the head. Mr. Crookshank and Mrs. Crookshank were taking pictures the whole time. But when Mrs. Crookshank saw the yearling get hit in the head and killed, she fainted and fell off the top of the chute into her husband's arms. And I was so humiliated—I don't remember what I did.

I learned right then and there that you only take deer out of the corral at night. You use lights to manage them. That's what I did later on. You blind them and they trot into the crate. But most importantly I learned not to let people, especially professional photographers, watch me while I was emptying the corral. After that, every Christmas for half a dozen years I got a Christmas card from the Crookshanks addressed simply to "The Deer Slayer."

James Simmons's Life Ever Lasting

Bulls Island has a large and somewhat unique population of black fox squirrels. Tradition had it they were all descended from a pair of squirrels caught on the mainland by Mr. Dominick's stable boy and released on the island. Though a fox squirrel's coloration can range from gray to black, these two happened to be black thus the genetic basis for the "black" fox squirrel's presence. My father, William P. Baldwin Jr., arriving late in the 1930s had accepted this story and entered it into his assistant refuge manager's reports where it remained as the official version until Gene Wood, a forestry professor, went in search of the Dominick's fabled stable boy and found James Simmons living close by the island's Moore's Landing entrance. Simmons, then eighty-three or eight-four, had actually been a young man when he was in charge of the stables, but he had been there from the start of Dominick's residency. He denied releasing any squirrel, saying, "When I go to Bulls, I meet de fox squirrel dare . . . Dem be plenty. Dem be everywhere."

Wood thought Simmons's version the correct one, since the normally low birth rate of the squirrels made it unlikely that a pair released in the mid 1920s could have increased to the hundreds found when the government bought the refuge from Mr. Dominick a decade later. Wood sent a copy of the memo to my father who passed it on to me. The memo remarked on Simmons's kindness, soundness of mind and ability as a conversationalist. I read that, called Gene Wood, who turned out to share many of my interests, and he was happy to direct me to James Simmons—which brings us to the beginning of this story.

Simmons Hill is a dirt lane near Bulls Island's Moore's Landing, and James Simmons's house is the first one you come to. A small cabin, it leans against a solid squat chimney. To one side is a cornfield, and tied out back is a small mule. At the door I explain that I've heard James worked on

Bulls Island as a young man, and I'd like to ask a few questions. He welcomes me, and we sit on a narrow, screened porch. For eighty-four, he's surprisingly fit. Graying hair at the temples. A ready smile. Suspenders hold up green double-knit trousers.

His wife Patsy sits to one side. Her dress is pale lavender with a flowered print, and she wears a plaid Scotch cap pulled across her hair. James leaves us. He's stepping out to the road to pick two lunches being delivered by the county health service. Patsy tells me she's been sick the last four years, not able to get around. She says she was raised over around Iron Swamp, Witherspoon to be exact. Her people were Cooper River people. James, too, had been from off, but he'd been raised here on the edge of Sewee Bay. She says little more, at least, at first. While I talk to her husband, she will sit quietly with her eyes closed. Still, she is listening and when his memory is short she often fills in the gaps.

James returns and begins to tell me about Bulls Island. He went over there in about 1925 to work for Mr. Dominick. They built dikes. Dominick had "contract come" and put in piling in the soupiest places. These were filled with sand bags. The rest of the dike work was done with wheelbarrows. They built Summer House bank from scratch but some ponds were already built. "We meet ponds there," he explains.

Mr. Dominick came only in the winter. "He don't see mosquito at t'all." His main interest was duck hunting hence the pond building. During the season James had other duties.

"Dominick ain't use them wood McCoy duck. He put duck live. You drop anchor. And duck on a line, have a halter. 'Quack, quack, quack!'" He mimics and chuckles. "Shoot them off the wing. Don't allow them shoot on the water."

Deer hunting was James's favorite. No dogs. The men drove them to the stands. "Clap you hand, lick at palmetto." Turkey hunting was another. Dominick stocked the island, and James recalls one turkey gobbler in particular. He raises his palm about four feet above the floor. "Big old turkey. Kill a mule. Had to spur um to kill um. Man bring a picture of the dead mule along with the turkey. Dominick want to change the breed we turn that turkey out, then we take the horse and wagon and haul tail back." Though this is said with a laugh, he shakes his head to indicate that this particular turkey was a creature to be reckoned with.

Dominick also turned loose quail. James thought the ticks had killed these. They also set out pheasant. "Didn't see too much of them. Can't stand the climate."

Though not for sport—or for any other reason he knew—they also had released sheep. He remembers one particularly big broad-horned ram named Jersey City that he rowed over there to "cross the blood." The sheep did well but were too wild to catch. Cows were there when they came, but these had to be shot because they were too dangerous. The bulls would smell your tracks if you walked the beach. "They get your scent like a dog and come at you. They holler." James makes a loud call, "Who-all, who-all. Them hear that, them better bush theyselves then [climb a tree]." The ladies couldn't go out so they shot all the cows.

Dominick had three houses built, the big Dominick house and two "good ones" for the servants, one of which is now a garage. They "meet the cottage house" when they got there. That last was from Mr. Clarence Magwood's time and was torn down. They also tore down the lighthouse keeper's house on the north end of the island. He recalls that it was pegged together. The metal light tower was still standing but well out in the sea, and Jack's Creek had broken through into the ocean as well.

I asked about the stable. "I saddle horse and surrey for White folks," and he adds the names of a few of his charges. "Lucky Strikes, Diggidity, Coco, Pet, a mule called Jane, a sensible mule." This last reminds him of his own mule now grazing behind the house. "A little Jack. I keep him for what he done. Don't want to see no mule killed."

Did the flies bother the stock? The stables were all screened and he dipped the stock in a cattle vat and sprayed them too, but the deerflies and mosquitoes still gave animals a bad time. "Couldn't see down the road for the mosquitoes. Kill about thee snakes between here and that house." He motions across the cornfield, a distance of about one hundred fifty feet. "Rattlesnakes, pilot and moccasins. Coil right by the side of the road." Still no one was ever killed and only one man was bit while he was there.

I asked about the old "Spanish" fort on the island's north end. He knows little about it. People dug there. They claimed "Rebel money" was buried there but found no money or anything else.

Did he remember the sailing freight boats? He did. "The first time I see that Bay there, the old *Betty* from Georgetown going by." Saying this he motions out from the porch and across the highway to a dense thicket of young pines, and I realize though the view is blocked, we are actually sitting close by the Bay's edge. The *Betty* had to use the Bulls narrow channel. The waterway hadn't been built through here until 1927. "They dredge the Congaree. Same year we married." He also remembered my grandfather Rutledge Leland's diesel powered *Carolina.* "Bootsie the captain." Bootsie was a light-skinned fellow and his brother the engineer was dark skinned. They taught James and Sam Whitesides how to load a boat when the two young men were running the *Heron* (a small freight boat) back and forth to Bulls Island. Sam was the engineer and James was the captain. "So-called captain," he laughs. "Bootsie would smoke pipe all night. Ain't ever sleep. As a matter you can't do too much sleeping on the water. Can't be a hard sleeper on a boat." Freight boat landings were all along the coast.

I asked if he remembered plumers—hunters taking the shore birds for their tail feathers—ever working the Bulls Bay area and he says no. When he was young you could still gather sea turtle eggs and bird eggs too, but they stopped that just before Mr. Dupre came to the island. (He was the first refuge manager at Bulls Island.) "Five hundred dollar fine now."

Did he ever pick oysters for a living? No. When he was a boy they scratched clams for the Magwoods and got 12¢ a water bucket. Had to row them over to Bulls. "Ain't no stern motor." The Shellmore Company had the oyster leases running all the way to Goat Island near Charleston, but no, James didn't turn to the water.

He left Bulls Island just before the government bought it and worked for the Tuxberry Lumber Company—then for the Atlantic Coastline and North Side Lumber too. "Was the Depression, not much money." There were logging trains running all through the woods. "Worked a place called Hell Hole, Dog Swamp, Sutler place—you wouldn't know where you were even if you climb a tree." They'd worked all the way to the Santee River. He'd cut on Bowman's Peachtree. The work was from dawn to dark. Tent camps were placed along the side of the tracks, but some people "had to sleep under the shade of the tree." You spent a week in the woods and walked home on the weekends, sometimes twenty-five miles or more.

We leave the lumbering days and return to earlier times. Cattle were raised all around Moore's Landing. They fed on the marsh and sometimes bogged so bad they couldn't get out. Those were eaten. His family lived right here on the "beach coast." (At least, in this end of Charleston County "the beach" is the marsh edge.) He was born right by the water. His daddy rented three acres of land. He farmed a little and caught jobs around. He'd worked in McClellanville for Hepburn Morrison. In his family they hadn't caught fish for money. They caught them for food. When he was young they casted from a bateau, picked clams and oysters on the shore and fished with hook and line. "All choice food."

Catching terrapin was something they did do for money. The Magwoods bought them and paid by the inch. "You track um in the marsh. They settle in a little pond. Scoop um up. Some people had puppies—would trail them in the marsh. You train your puppy. You hear um bark." Raccoons were also trapped in the marsh of the Bay because they destroyed the birds. Dan Taylor did that.

Though not so much for employment, they burnt oyster shells for lime, made shingles and split rails. James's wife teases that his rail-splitting days are gone. "Know how, ain't able," he agrees. Not all occupations are exhausted, but I next ask James and Patsy if they remember the hurricane of 1916. After talking it over, they both agree that they don't. We are about to pass on to other subjects when Patsy adds that the only hurricane she remembered was the storm of 1911. James said, yes, he was young but he remembers that one too. "I ain't just been here. My old man step out the bed. Step in the water." They woke everyone up and waded to high ground. His daddy had been so frightened for his family's safety that he'd forgotten about his horse and so had to wade back and open the stable door. The horse swam out. The water came that high. All the clothes on the lines blew away and the watermelons floated far up into the woods. After the storm was worse, though. "You couldn't walk the edge of the beach. Stink. Sedge and dead birds. And big boats pop loose and was up in the woods all along the beach cost. Some ain't have the money. Have to let the boat stay there. King family, all them could repair boat. A poor person can't do it."

This leads us back to occupations or at least money saving measures. Did he remember shell being burned for lime? "Burn right here on the beach. Put lime in the fields. Sieve it out and build your chimney. Whitewash your house." The shell was burned by making a pen of split saplings, like a pig pen, then you piled the shell up inside and out and fired the wood. "Do em at night. No children around then. Shell will pop. Shoot like a gun. So burn em after dusk dark."

The rail splitting for cattle fencing was something he did plenty of too. His wife teases again that his rail splitting days are over. Splitting shingles was something else he could do. "Straight grain yellow pine. Could cut out a shingle longer than you if you want em. Tell by the grain. Can't use no short leaf pine."

Salt making? No. They both agree that ended before they were born. "Last old man boil salt buried down there," James points down the road. "All the hammocks, anyplace high along the marsh, that's where they make salt."

At this point his brother William steps up onto the porch. Twenty years younger, he still has a pretty good idea of "the old times." I ask both brothers about the moonshine business. They answer that it was easy work for those that did it. Just keeping a fire going was about it, but nobody who did that ever saved any money. "If you work hard, you know where your money go," James says. William agrees and adds, "Them fellow on the shrimp boat, they got an easy job. So end of the year ain't got nothing."

This discussion of hard-earned money leads us to the subject of bill paying: light bills and phone bills. Patsy adds insurance, because you have to have something to be buried with. William says, "In the old days just took lumber—ripped lumber out of the loft of an abandoned house and pay the carpenter three or four dollars, if you got it, to build a coffin that night." A mixture of soot, kerosene and egg painted the box.

"Look like a bought casket," James adds.

"Sometimes could get cloth and a little tack," Patsy says. A wagon and a horse took you to the cemetery, but this somber reflection leads immediately to the cure of illnesses. The nearest doctor was fifteen or twenty miles away, but the old people knew the herbs. James points outside. "Herb tree, that a good one. That holly bush." An avalanche of information follows.

"Life Ever Lasting—you boil um. Sweat the fever out of you." James steps off the porch and returns to give me a ragged, leafy stalk. I'm not sure of the spelling or pronunciation, but there were other herbs. Rizlen was mostly just to drink as a tea. Sassafras—you dug the roots during the winter and dried them, but it couldn't be drunk during certain summer months. (Surprisingly, they'd never had cassena tea or at least didn't identify it by that name.) Snakeroot they felt was such an obvious and well-known cure it didn't bear discussion. Patsy says that Flatgrass made a tea. She also mentions "Satisfat" but that might have been her name for Sassafras.

William seemed to know the plants discussed so far, but he has to return to work. We say goodbye and then return to the discussion of herbs. Both James and Patsy insist I understand that the plants we are discussing can no longer be used as medicine because they are drugs. "You can go to a doctor, but in them times got no doctor. Now can't find no root doctor around here."

Dogwood tea was good for a fever. Life Ever Lasting was best mixed with the boiled leaves of holly. "Broke a fever. But best don't put sugar in most of these teas when you use em for sickness." Putting sugar in an herb tea made it simply a tea. Bitter Bush made another good tea. "Mongol Bush old-time people call it." For backache, pine-top tea was good. "Get a pine the height of you. Get the limb, break off just the top. Boil the stick and all. Must be long-leaf pine. Short-leaf just good for tea."

Dr. Frampton, a Mt. Pleasant doctor who had treated them, would always laugh and say, "You left all the medicine behind you," meaning that the cures were in the woods. There was also an herb doctor in Mt. Pleasant who, if you paid him, would tell you what to gather. The herb doctor especially recommended the water from the overflow pump, an artesian well on the beach.

"Water good for you," James says.

"Taste too bad, rotten egg," Patsy says.

"Sulfur" James says and then goes on. "Dogwood is bitter as gall. Lot of that around in from the beach. Not here. Old root lady learned me a lot once. Might get the wrong stuff. Not put it together." This is another warning to me and then he goes on. "When you see a black snake around a root, that a fever root. He will eat it."

Patsy mentions pine gum, and her husband says you make pills from the gum. "Punch them out. For back trouble you swallow them. Roll them around in your hand, make a pill." Patsy expresses doubt, but her husband insists, "That back ain't going to worry you again. I try them." Another cure for back pain is made from a root that runs across the road. "Can't be too much traffic. One of the old, blind roads. Got to be two-way traffic. Chop the root where the wagon hit it. Skin off and boil it and make a plaster, put that on your back. Draw um up tight. Can draw um up too tight. One night my daddy have to tear um off." James pantomimes his father tearing off the plaster. We laugh. "Anything in the woods is good," James concludes. "Green moss good for neck trouble. Wrap it, stay here till dry."

Patsy shakes her head in contradiction and says she "never try um."

James says, "Green moss and mullet—make a paste and put it on any pain. That's the old folks' way."

Patsy says, "That's the old folks' way."

As if on cue, the county's rural health nurse is at the door—come to check her over. And Patsy seems content enough to be placed in the hands of twentieth-century medicine. To give her privacy James and I leave the porch and step into the backyard. I ask him if he has ever heard about the attempt made by the freed slaves to buy Bulls Island. He says no. He only knows one slave story about Bulls Island, and that one is about Old Man Bluebeard. I listen.

"Old Man Bluebeard—he have a beard just like you, but the beard blue. He was partly a slave man. Lots of people staying over on Bulls. He trick um over there. They living here on de mainland, and he bring a boat and have banjo-playing on the boat, the people say. The people go to hear the banjo. When you look back, he done eased the boat off, and you couldn't get away—so this must be slavery times.

"Old Bluebeard—even though he was a slave, he was the boss, and when you get old, he wouldn't let you eat up the grocery. Some place they take care of you. On Bulls they had a thing down Jack's Creek. Tub of acid.

"Bluebeard go to Jack one morning, say, 'Got one for you kill.' Jack a big man, got arms that big round." James Simmons held out his forearm and circled it with an open palm. "Was a strong man. Bluebeard say, 'I want you to kill my mother.'

"Jack say, 'You gonna kill your mama?'

"Bluebeard say, 'She ain't working. Ain't no feed for the rest of um.'

"Jack ain't want to do it. He worry about it all night, but he had to get up the next morning and kill Bluebeard's mama. Then the next morning Bluebeard came to Jack and say, 'Now, you got to kill your Mama.'"

The story is over. With a surprising suddenness. Needless to say James is an animated story teller and a joy to listen to. But I'm a scholar of sorts, a pedant of sorts and as I listened I'd been breaking the tale down into myth and morality. The Jack stories are English derived and found by the hundreds in the Appalachian Mountains. Bulls Island's Jack's Creek was actually named for Mr. Jackson, a lumberman. The banjo playing was done in Africa not at Moore's Landing. Bluebeard was the killer of wives. Blackbeard was the blood-thirsty pirate who had supposedly come ashore on Bulls Island. Bits of traditional folklore were mixed with history and the result was a tale the likes of which I'd never heard or read before.

James's second story is shorter and certainly more direct.

"When I went on the island they show me where they hang up people on Jack's Creek. Broke their neck. On the first landing road was where the trees were. They show me the limbs they hang the people on. They ain't seen um, people show them. They show me. Ain't no rule then. People do as they choose. People still do as they choose someplaces."

I nodded in agreement and we're joined in the backyard by James's nephew. I miss his name in the introduction. He's a thin man. Thirty-eight years old. He wears a cap that says "Vietnam Vet and Proud of It." A discussion of that war follows. James laughs and says he was drafted at the end of WWI, but the war was over three days later and he was glad to get home. This leads to a discussion of the nearby Civil War battle at Andersonville. James says he farmed there and found unexploded shells in the fields and in the marsh. He'd been told "a ship throw em there." I mention that the Black infantry had landed there. The nephew knows of the Black troops in the Civil War. He speaks then of the Buffalo Soldiers and also mentions the record of a particular New York division.

The old man goes to restake his mule, and his nephew asks what bush I'm holding. It's the Life Ever Lasting given to me when I first arrived, but I've forgotten the name and can only hold it up.

"That," the nephew says, "you mix that with a little lemon and gin. That's all we ever had for fever."

James comes back and I say goodbye to the two of them and then go home and tell my wife, Lil, all about my conversation with James, Patsy and William. I tell her James's nephew is only thirty-eight and he's been raised taking Life Ever Lasting tea.

My wife says that doesn't surprise her. Though her father was a pharmacist and her mother a nurse, she was raised for the most part by a local Black woman who knew the herbal remedies. She, too, is thirty-eight and she and her sisters were constantly being patched up with a mixture of dog spit and cobwebs. Though she doesn't think she ever drank Life Ever Lasting, she was often told of its healing properties.

Hearing this I see no alternative but to crumple my sample into a pot of boiling water. Steeped and poured into a cup, the liquid is the color of ordinary tea, but slightly opaque. I sip. The taste is like that of many herb teas that come packaged on supermarket shelves, but there is an extra tang. A weedy taste, a taste of August, of broom sedge, dust and roadside. The taste of Simmons Hill. I sit, drink and feel relaxed and imagine, at least, that I am a little lightheaded.

Yes. Life Ever Lasting is certainly a name rich in promise. Early in our conversation, James Simmons had explained to me about names. "Some names you don't know where they come from. You just meet um when you get here."

Originally published in *charleston* magazine

Bucky Hills

I talked to Bucky in the late 1980s and typed the piece up a few years later. This is the first time it's been in print.

WHILE DOING THESE INTERVIEWS BUCKY Hills's name had come up several times. He'd worked on Bulls Island from 1940 to 1946. Before that and afterward he'd worked close by on the mainland. He was now seventy-three years old. He'd been sick, had poor circulation and his left leg had been amputated below the knee. But he still got around. I met him on the steps of the Presbyterian church after a service and asked if I could visit. He said I was welcome. He was living in a trailer behind his son's house near Cainhoy. I must take the Halfway Creek road to where it hits Highway 41.

Well, I thought there were faster ways to Cainhoy (I was wrong) but he'd insisted on the Halfway Creek way, which was just as well, for it would serve as a good introduction to what followed. I was vaguely familiar with the terrain. Sabe Cumbee, the most notorious of the Berkeley County bootleggers, is buried here in a tiny country graveyard that any saint would envy. And this section of the county had been settled three hundred years before by the shipwrecked Presbyterians of Wappetaw. This last point Bucky mentions when I'm seated and ask him exactly where we are. The landing used by those 1697 pioneers was at Andersonville and the road ran straight up to Wappetaw Church, which is behind the Sewee store (now a restaurant) and about eight miles from us as the crow flies. He recommends I read the few remaining church records and then the conversation moves on to Bulls Island.

"During the war," he says, "we found that submarines were putting Germans off on the island. We had a man penned up. We asked for help and the navy sent up a bunch of game wardens." (A slightly different version from my father's, who claimed they sent a corp of Marines but sent them a month after the request.) Bucky says his cousin Roy Hills had been filling in the Moccasin Pond bank. "They looked up and this fellow in a business suit carrying a briefcase walked by in broad daylight. The fellow with Roy ran, so Roy tried to trail the man from a distance. He figured the man knew what he was doing—knew where he was going. Finally Roy found a place on the back of the island, a place of beachy sand and he dug down and found warm ashes of a fire buried. There were cigarette butts there, some with rouge, which meant one person was a woman. They figured the man met some kind of boat there. Figured that he'd been let off of a German submarine and come ashore as a spy. Stories were going around like that. A man up in Darien, Georgia, got arrested for selling fuel to the German subs."

In my father's version of the story they were trapping turkeys when the German spy walked by, which leads me into asking about the animal trapping on Bulls Island—the idea that a wildlife refuge could be used to generate wildlife for other areas.

Bucky said, "I was catching coons for West Virginia and Virginia. Sold them live for restocking there." He'd worked with a Black fellow over there, a man named Issah Whitesides who was called "Doggie." "Doggie was a double-jointed fellow with hands as big as dishpans. I'd find the coon sleeping in a tree. Shine the eyes. Issah would climb the tree and knock them down with his bare hands. I'd throw the net over them, little wire net with a pipe handle. Got good at it. Didn't miss."

Deer trapping? "This fellow Griffin came up from Florida to trap deer. Couldn't catch them. He'd make a path to the trap. Put the trap out with his bare hand. I'd tell him not to do that. The deer would smell him. I can still see your daddy smiling watching him do that. Griffin didn't catch a single deer. He went back to Florida and joined the army, which was what he wanted to do anyway."

Turkey trapping? "Turkey eggs seemed to come in odd numbers—seven, nine, thirteen. Once I did find eighteen, most I found and the only even number. I got the eggs and hatched them out on the island. Lots of things after the nest. Crows came right down and ate them as they hatched. I'd run them off. They got big enough the young could roost in trees. Owls would try and get them but the old turkey hen would put her wing over the brood."

Leaving Bulls Island? "They offered me a job as manager [warden] on the Santee Lakes, but I didn't trust those Berkeley County people. They'd just shot the manager's eye out. I wasn't going to let them shoot me. Anyway, after the war a new man came and they accused me of hunting turkeys on the island. I said, 'I ain't killed a fiddler over there.' I even drove up to Atlanta and argued. In 1947 I quit and went to work as a forester up here at Cainhoy on the plantation of Harry Guggenheim. His daddy had made a woodstove polish, then bought on the Cooper. A Cooper King. After that I went with the CCC's in Francis Marion National Forest. They'd carved that out of Berkeley County wilderness."

Were the woods clear-cut before the forest was established? "No. They were mature trees growing. Sixteen inches or bigger. The problem back then was burning. The Berkeley County residents didn't own the land but they kept burning it like they did 'cause they wanted their cattle to have the green shoots coming up in the spring. They'd get on mule back and ride through the woods with a box of kitchen matches throwing them out or they'd tie a couple of burning sacks behind the mule and ride them through the woods. One of my first jobs with the CCC's, I was to hide and catch one of these people." Bucky laughed at this and shook his head. "They'd carried me down in some God forsaken place and left me. Once a man did come by on a mule with a couple of ornery looking dogs, but he wasn't lighting fires. I stayed hidden and I'd have stayed hidden even if he was lighting fires. Back then they'd kill you in Berkeley County."

What was his next job? "My Uncle Dick [my great-uncle R.L. Morrison] was running the CCC crew, which was made up of a lot of boys from New Jersey. Rough fellows. They'd pick up a copperhead and put it live in their pockets. Judge would give them a choice of going to the penitentiary or going to the CCC camp in South Carolina. My next job was being put in the first fire tower that was built. This was on the Halfway Creek road about five miles up toward Awendaw. [I'd driven by the spot that morning.] They'd built this little house up on poles about as high as a telephone pole. A week on and a week off was the schedule. This was a good job except one of the first fires I reported lead to trouble. I saw fire and smoke. Turned out to be a big whiskey still, a double decker with electric lights. The CCC boys got all the whisky they could haul. They were drunk. There were a couple of three hundred- to four hundred-pound hogs there drunk from eating the mash. The boys took the hogs and put them in the army commander's cabin and when the hogs came to they tore the sides off the house. The captain came to me mad and I told him my job was to report smoke.

"'Course the important complaint come from the bootleggers. They said they were going to shoot me. I carried a mattress up there in the little house and put it over the trap door. Had two or three guns, a shotgun and two rifles. They came the next morning at daylight and I shouted down I had them covered and hollered that the other fellows with me should hold their fire. Of course, I was alone. They wanted to know why I'd reported them. I pointed out I didn't have any way of knowing it was a still. We made a deal. If they'd tell me where their still was I wouldn't report it. Sometimes after that if it was a clear day I'd see the smoke from thirty stills."

His brother Beckett Hills? "They had some contrary game wardens back then, but Beckett was a particularly contrary poacher. He'd shoot a doe out of season and out of bounds and then leave its head sticking on a post. He got arrested once by John McClellan for hunting turkeys inside the government pasture (the closed part of the forest). Beckett said he'd only go on the condition that John 'tote him out.' John said, 'You damn well know I won't tote you.' So Beckett went unarrested."

Did Bucky ever hunt with his brother? "We'd hunt up on the Santee Delta. One time Beckett talked me into letting him off on the north end of Murphy Island and picking him up on the south end. There were supposed to be two bad fellows from Texas watching the island. I waited in Alligator Creek, anchored close to the shore. I could hear the sound of the shotguns coming closer and closer. Finally, here comes Beckett. He breaks from the woods. He's coming through the marsh trailing a long rope. He's got twenty-nine geese and ducks tied on it and right behind him is the watchman grabbing at the rope. But Beckett climbs in the boat and pulls the rope in after him and we leave the man there cussing us."

Other hunting stories? "John McClellan was hunting wild hogs, had a permit and had the dogs. Dogs trained to do that. The catch dog was on a string. The other dogs bay the hog. The catch dog got him by the ear. Then you catch the hog by the hind legs and hold him before he gets you. We sold them live.

"Alligators was another business John was in but that was illegal and I wasn't with him on that. In Waterhorn they took a thousand hides. Didn't worry about the law. He had two others with him. I was cutting post in there, heart pine and cypress fence post. We knew they were killing them but couldn't find the carcasses. One day I saw them climb a fence and saw them shoot. They skinned the gator where they shot him and buried the carcass right there. No sign."

Bucky's wife joins us. We say hello. She says she hasn't seen me since I was a child. I say I have grown sons now. She and Bucky have five great-grandchildren, two in school already. Then a remark she makes leads us around to my uncle, Wewa Leland. After he left Bulls Island, Bucky had briefly gone to work for my uncle as a boat captain. Wewa had hired him to deliver the *North Star* to New York. He'd sold her to somebody up there. The *North Star* was a deluxe rumrunner. Or had been. She came from New York originally and was the same boat that Dick Stall had escaped from. Bucky said she'd seen better days.

"She was leaking bad and once we got going I discovered that Wewa had stripped the boat of anything that had value. No life jackets. Of course not.

He robbed everything. Just left enough to make the engine turn over. No water pumps, he even took the generator off the side and the spare batteries. I got to North Carolina before the battery gave out. Had to paddle the boat up to the dock. Your uncle gave us $300 expense money and I knew that was all the money we were going to see. There was only one thing left on the boat. A spotlight. I traded that for a battery charge. Another place they just gave us a charge. We got into Norfolk after a week. I called the man in New York and said, 'We are very ill.' He sent a fellow down. He got the boat halfway across the Chesapeake Bay and it sank there. We rode the Greyhound bus home."

This leads to another Wewa story and then to a reminiscence of his brother Beckett holding five game wardens at gunpoint. "You know Beckett was like that from boyhood. When he and Bill Graham shot the shingle roof out of the society's clubhouse, J.B. Morrison signed a warrant against him. J.B. was about the only one who could handle him."

J.B. Morrison is our common ancestor—Bucky's great-uncle and my great-grandfather. Does Bucky remember him? "Remember him well. Little short fellow, old, old, gray beard, drove around in a buggy, then he had a Model T. He was an orator, a stump speaker. He could draw a crowd. Once, the police couldn't arrest a Negro they went after. They got J.B. and he just pointed his walking stick at the man and he came out his house. Surrendered."

This leads into a discussion of hunting at the Morrison's Doe Hall, but a friend of Bucky's arrives. He wants to carry him out to look for signs of poaching on some land they've leased.

I say my goodbyes and drive back along the Halfway Creek road. But this time I turn in at the Apple Hill Cemetery. The little sandy knoll is surrounded by a thick forest of young pines. I don't see the apple tree, but this is a place of beauty and a place of total quiet. Sabe Cumbee is buried here.

Sabe Cumbee didn't die until 1968, which is far, far longer than a lot of people had intended. This "King of Hellhole" was one of the principal moonshiners, an occupation that came with considerable risks. The story goes (one of many) that back in the 1930s he'd been ambushed somewhere nearby. His son, sitting beside him in the car, was killed and Sabe was shoot in the chest with buckshot. But he drove himself up to the hospital in Moncks Corner. When the doctor wanted to put him under with the anesthetic, Sabe is supposed to have said, "The buckshot came in while I was awake and they're coming out the same way."

Leaving Apple Hill Cemetery, I cross over the Moncks Corner highway and stay on the Halfway Creek road until I come to the mission church. Abandoned now, the little building dates from the Depression and was meant to serve the entire community. Oddly enough my parents had been instrumental in its founding. I'd been lightly connected to it myself. Sixteen years before, Pauline Ackerman had brought my wife Lil and me here because she was about to have a cataract operation and she thought she would die. I hadn't paid close attention at the time, but I see now her family is buried here along with dozens of others. But the entire community of Halfway Creek was condemned during WWII. The area was so isolated and impoverished it was a problem (an embarrassment) for county officials and apparently the solution had been to use it as a bombing range. Most of the residents moved in closer to McClellanville.

I leave the church and drive on to Honey Hill. I pass the small black water pond that Pauline told us was bottomless. "A cow fall in that," she said, "it fall forever." I go twenty miles without passing a single car. But a few people are settled here, scattered out in the woods. Still, it's wilderness enough and an area I've always thought of as a dangerous place (though on this spring afternoon it seems peaceable enough). Bucky Hills spent a good bit of his life around here, and he seemed to think so too. Getting shot by Berkeley County people had been a primary concern of his. But then I'm separated from him by thirty years of road building and forest management by the U.S. government. Gentler times have come.

At Palmer Bridges, I cross back over the Berkley County line. Near here Mr. Sullivan and his horse are supposed to be buried side by side. And long years ago Mr. McKay was shot at this bridge, murdered and robbed by persons unknown. Swamp on one side of the county line and swamp on the other. A homogenized society. The chance of having your eye shot out has diminished considerably but spread itself out into the world at large.

Albertha Winn

ALBERTHA WINN WAS BORN IN 1910. Her family's place was just north of Palmetto Plantation, just inland from where the Shokes family had lived. It was in what I'd been told was called "Freedom Village," a Black community started after the Civil War and finally abandoned during the 1920s. Albertha calls it "The Beach."

"All this land along DuPre Road here. The water edge called the Beach. Up here on the road called the Beach. I ain't know why. Dat a name the old people give us."

I had come to ask Albertha about Cape Romain. To what degree had people once depended on the resources of the marshland in order to survive?

That was my question, one that for the purpose of such interviews, I had broken down into a dozen or so stock inquiries. How was lime made? How were oysters picked? Etc.

Alice DeAntonio went with me on this visit. Alice is my age (early baby boomer). A DuPre before marriage, her family's ties with the interviewee were long and cordial. Together we sat on the screened porch of Albertha's small house close to DuPre Road. This is a narrow paved highway that heads north of McClellanville paralleling the Cape Marsh, but inland about a half mile. A little ways down it turns to dirt, twists through the headwaters of Blake's reserve and eventually reaches the community of Collins Creek and beyond that the Old Santee Club. Albertha's life has been lived along this road. Sometimes at one end, sometimes the other. But always closely tied to the Cape itself.

"Oyster? Boy, my life ain't been nothing but oyster. I shuck oyster from when I was a little girl right on. I stop shucking oysters three years ago."

She has a gentle face and manner. Thin. Her husband Sam Winn died last year. She's been sick herself, and one of her sons has come from New York to look after her. She's happy for Alice's company, and I have my questions about "The Beach" area. Our conversation goes along these lines.

"Grant. Nesbitt. Singleton. Weston. De been five or six families living der." Ralf Nesbitt was her mama's daddy. Sam Grant was her daddy. Josephine Grant, her mama, shucked oysters for George Shokes who had a factory on the creek nearby.

The factory was a long house with a concrete floor. Albertha was the oldest of the children, and she'd gone to work there as a small child, standing beside her mother. She didn't know what they were paid then. Her mother kept the money. "Just give them a little something." In raw-shucking you don't steam the oysters open. You break off the tip with a heavy, thick-bladed oyster knife and work the blade back and sever the muscle. Since she grew up shucking, she got to be very fast. "I get one and half buckets. They get one." Shokes was a good man to work for, and when she was grown he would go off and leave her in charge.

The factory usually employed ten women, five standing on each side of the table. Albertha couldn't recall exactly how many men were working in the creek. Her grandfather oystered. Five or six others maybe. They worked Monday through Friday. The women had trouble keeping up with what was brought in. Sometimes a trip would keep them busy for two days. The bateaus came in loaded down low in the water, and the meat of the oysters back then was big, fat and "white as snow," nothing at all like what's being shucked today. "Beautiful oysters," she recalls. "Beautiful oysters."

I'd been looking at an aerial photograph of Palmetto Plantation and was curious about the rice fields. There had been one set of fields well inland on a section called "The Morass," and another had been built by an impoundment of the Cape salt marsh, the two joined together by a canal. Both had since been converted to duck ponds, which had been abandoned and gone dry in recent years. I asked Albertha about rice growing on Palmetto.

"Rice. Boy, you ain't never seen such rice." She remembered both sets of fields, and both were being planted when she was a girl. The rice was milled right there on the plantation, and corn was grown and milled right there too. Mr. DuPre was a good man. Generous to those who worked for him. He grew everything. Cotton, potatoes, sweet and white, peanuts, watermelon and cantaloupes.

But the DuPres weren't the only ones. The families in her settlement all farmed. They grew practically everything they needed to eat. Like the DuPres they raised chickens, cattle and hogs, and they killed wild turkeys and ducks. From the creek they got oysters, shrimp, crab and fish. Her daddy went striking for flounder with a pronged pole and a kerosene lantern.

Salt? Anywhere on the water you could make salt. You boiled it in an iron pot. The Shokes boiled saltwater there on the beach and sold the salt in little cloth bags. They had a store by the shucking house, "a shop" where you could get candy and a little groceries. But there wasn't much for sale. "Make we own corn, rice, salt, had sugar cane to take to the mill and then boil sugar. Buy a little green coffee. Some candy." George Shokes brought his store provisions on a freight boat all the way from Charleston.

Terrapin? Terrapin is "sweet meat." She remembers that they were measured under the stomach. Six inches and over were kept. There was no pen on the beach, but they were carried in tubs into the Village. "Terrapin? Everybody do that for a living."

Lime? Sure they made lime. You took "trash" out of the woods and some lightwood, too, and then piled the oyster shells on top of that, then poured fuel oil on it and let it burn. People came and bought it. "Make cement out of it. Good cement."

Roots? Medicine from the woods? Her daddy knew them all, but she didn't learn it. She remembers fever bush. The rest of it she didn't learn.

Canoes? Did anyone use cypress log canoes in the creeks? Yes. Her granddaddy and daddy each had log canoes that they used to go in the creek. These were canoes that had been burned and shaped with axes and adzes. On Sunday afternoons the children would be carried down to the beach edge to play in the water. She remembers sitting in a canoe paddling in the shallow water with her hands. "Boy," she says. "Don't ask me 'bout them canoes. Make me cry just to think about them." She is crying.

Albertha married Sam Winn when she was nineteen. He was fifteen years her senior and working as a duck hunting guide for Santee Club. (I'd seen his name mentioned there often in the records.) They had moved to the Blakes—her name for the Santee Club, which is now called the Santee Coastal Preserve. They lived there for a good while. Her husband paddled the men out to the blinds and liked his work. The members, "'des people from the North," were good to him, brought him winter clothes, shoes and socks. They would still come to get him when he and Albertha moved to the opposite end of DuPre Road. That was over now though. The Club had ended. The children of the old members weren't interested in hunting. "Dat young set just give it up."

We talked about other things. Her brother was Sonny Grant, whom I knew well. He had drowned about five years before casting for mullet. He was an epileptic, and most thought it was a seizure that had caused him to fall forward and follow the casted net off the edge of the dock. I speak not of that but of the night twenty-five years before. I was coming in from striking flounder. Sonny was running a shrimp boat called the *Fiddler* and we'd almost collided. His boat was at least thirty-five feet long and was taking up all of the channel, for he was towing the narrow island cut at least five miles inside any legal shrimping boundaries.

Albertha enjoys this story. She laughs and tells me that I am the man if I can remember the *Fiddler*. Alice speaks of their earlier times together. We are leaving. Albertha says our visit had made her spirits rise. We thank her and are gone.

I can't help thinking of Walker Percy's essay *The Message in the Bottle* when I've come away from such an encounter. (Actually, I haven't seen this essay in at least eight years. Either the author says this, or I dreamed he does.) Percy argues that the anthropologist is like the man who finds a message in a bottle that has floated up on a beach. It has floated across a vast ocean from a land that he can't even imagine. If he is not a part of a culture, then he lacks the intimacy to understand it. Conversely, if he is a member of that culture, then he lacks the detachment to judge in an analytical or scientific manner. In short, we can never know. What difference keeps me from really understanding Albertha's world? Race, education, class, sex, money all come to mind, but the most obvious problem is time. The thirty years that separates us have been the most progress-oriented in the history of the world. Mankind has taken its giant leap. Here on the Cape people have stopped planting rice, stopped shooting ducks, stopped raw-shucking oysters, stopped terrapinning, stopped boiling their salt and burning their lime. They've stopped planting Sea Island cotton and practically everything else. They've stopped living off the land and have often abandoned it all together.

Whether realistic or not, it seems natural for Albertha to look back on her childhood as a time of peace and security, a time when she was surrounded by family. There was plenty to eat and what you ate did not depend on the vagaries of a moneyed economy and the spending of a small social security check.

I look back on her childhood with similar hopes. I want to believe that for a generation or two, the citizens of "Freedom Village" had fallen back on the Cape marsh and used it much as the earlier Sewee Indians had—to live in sympathetic harmony with nature, taking what they needed of seafood and supplementing it with what they grew and hunted on the mainland. Apparently they did. Albertha is not the first to suggest this, but I'm uneasy about this conversation and most of the other interviews—White, as well as Black.

Almost to the present day, dug-out canoes have been used on the freshwater rivers of the Lowcountry, but had they ever actually been in the more expansive coastal areas like the Cape marshes? The folklorist at the McKissock Museum had asked me this question a year before. I had wondered myself and had already asked it of several others who could remember none there. The day before this conversation with Albertha, however, Alice's aunt, Helen DuPre Saterlee, had recalled the canoes being used in the salt creeks in front of Palmetto Plantation. A tree would be cut, she said, and the center chipped and burnt out. "Trust me Gaud" was the name given to them by the Black population because you had to trust God so you wouldn't flip over. Alice's aunt remembered, and Albertha did too, but there was an emotional element to the latter's answer, which had no counterpart in what was really only a clinical question. "Boy. Don't ask me 'bout them canoes. Make me cry just to think about them."

Not long after this interview I built a little house on the exact site of the Shokes raw-shucking house. The mosquitoes and deer flies were so bad the bank inspectors wouldn't even get out of their car. I remember them pressing their faces against the glass and looking up. I guess they wanted to make sure the roof was on.

I built the house for Jean Edwards, a woman whose Connecticut parents had homesteaded the property back in the 1940s. Her father gave up a stock advice newsletter he'd been writing and came with his wife to watch birds. The cabin they moved into had neither electricity nor plumbing. Jean loved birds, as well. So does my fellow editor Elizabeth "the ruthless" Turk. She lives in Jean's house now. Birds scramble about her feeders. Starlings and red wing black birds for the most part, but obligatory cardinals come and buntings, too.

I can't step into that yard without thinking of Albertha Winn shucking those "white as snow oysters" and boiling the creek water down to salt.

Originally published in *View* magazine

Will Alston Speaks of Hampton

I bumped into Will Alston out at Hampton Plantation one day back in the 1980s. I hadn't intended to interview him, but as we walked around Hampton I took these brief notes. Archibald Rutledge was the state's poet laureate and through his poetry, essays and tales he made Hampton Plantation world famous. He was greatly indebted to the storytelling ability of the plantation's Blacks, especially to the Alston family, and happily acknowledged their help. Will Alston was the last of the Hampton storytellers. He died not long after our encounter. For not going back with a tape recorder—for not taking the time to really listen—I could kick myself. There's poetry here of the highest order. Archibald would have called these "words from the heart."

JONES WAS THE FERRYMAN. HE run the flat across the Santee. That the only way to get to Georgetown. Charleston a long way off. We got farming at Hampton. Sweet potatoes, rice, anything you can make. Turpentine sometimes. Sign on and off turpentine camp. I ain't remember the turpentine. Remember the oak barrels they keep um in. I got shingle though.

Sam Alston my great uncle. He make the old people laugh. Somebody say, "Did you hear about Kaiser?" He say, "I'm the man who kill Kaiser." He lie. They talking about Lindberg. Man fly the airplane. They say the first man put a plane over sea. He say, "He gone but he ain't gonna make." Sam Alston telling that to old man Banno. That the old man who could get out shingle. Cut em. Take the crosscut saw and cut down on the stump. Measure with a stick. That after the tree done cut. They come behind and make shingle. Chop out the shingle. They make brick too. I just a little boy. Grandfather dig down to clay. Still making brick on Hampton.

Spring water. We drink spring water on Hampton. Horry first man to find the spring so we tote water from Horry spring. I help my daddy tote the water. We got another spring. Montgomery spring. That Indian spring. By little bridge. Colored church was there. Up on the hill. Left hand coming in. Rattlesnake killed. Threw it in. People 'fraid the water. That by the St. James sign.

Hampton been the Horry place. Horry the first wife. Brought my great grandfather from Horry [came with her at the time of the marriage]. Rutledge married into Hampton. Great grandfather tell grandfather. After the war nobody go in that Hampton house and bother them women.

Indians? Last place for the Indians on the hill. We down at Blakes having picnic. We want to play. Old people want to tell us about Indians. "See that hill yonder," they say. "Play ball," we say. "That was the last place they had the chief Indians," they say. The old people trying to tell us and we just play. That hill down at Blakes, back this side of Gun Club. People still staying there. That house ain't burn [Union troops?] My grandfather tell me bunch of men coming dressed in brown clothes. See them coming in two shifts.

Slavery time. Slaves staying in Waterhorn. Old man German was the first Black man to come over here [Germantown]. They name town after him.

Hunting? I remember game warden tell em [his father], "Against the law to shoot rice birds." He lean gun against the tree. Say, "Won't get a mouthful. They eat up all." Oh, we camp out all 'bout this place. Hunt down as far as Bulls Island. Mostly duck. We hunt deer. Everything. Camp out. Spend many night. I shoot. "Hear one shot ain't no more." They say that about me. Don't shoot no does. Boy don't run like a girl. Spot just a spike. Can't see em. Boy run with the head straight up. Girl head straight out. Shoot wild hog, too.

Alligator? Shoot him in the head. Shoot him in the stomach. White people won't believe. We bait the hook. Big alligator follow tide in and set the hook. "Set the hook!" they shouting. "Talk like a man!" "Making fire," they say. "Knock on the boss man's door!" That gator pulling them in. "Molly!" Bunch of people come there. "Put hand on the line!" Gay Myer shout. "Pop the gator in head!" That the biggest I seen. Fourteen and half feet. Biggest in the freshwater.

Bury standing up? [the burial at nearby Peachtree] Bury he son standing up. Man who sign the Declaration of Independence do that. 'Nother one. Snyder Hill. Snyder buried standing up. Somebody stole the stone off of Snyder.

We cemetery. [local] Pipe and old coffee cup on grave. Got them thing like chewing tobacco can marking grave. Going back through to great grandfather time. They put them to your head. All them stolen off the grave. I remember old man Sambo Green. He set up all night building the coffin. Work in the lamp light, the lantern light. Could hear em. Get white piece of cloth and take that top and bottom.

'Nother carpenter. That the cook on the boat, the steamboat. He boarding with my mother. He say he going to make push wagon. "What kind of push wagon?" Say like they start a fight. He get saw and cut down pine and saw out the wheel. Get a big nail, let it get hot, knock it. Take a little auger open it up. Got a push wagon. Everybody build em. Children started making them. "Watch now," he say. "Cars gonna get built." They laugh at him. Them children never seen a car.

I remember old man White. That a colored man the people won't believe. Buzzards eating a cow. A whole flock. Boys want to play ball. Have a glove on he hand. Mr. White say, "Children, y'all see yonder. The time coming when man gonna fly in the air. Twenty head of children laugh. Children laugh. He take he hat off and stick it in he mouth he so mad. Hadn't been six months they hear that Mr. Lindburg go over seas. Them hear the old man. I don't know. Them believe he tell a damn lie. Man can't go over the sea. Lindburg was the first White man to go over sea. After that they could see the plane. One plane broke. Came right down in the field by them. Cornfield. Stay three days. Rutledge was in Spartanburg. He came back then. The man going pay for the corn. He tell them that was all right. Head man gave him bunch of tobacco.

Jones was the ferryman. Run the flat across the Santee. Only way to get to Georgetown. Charleston way off. Steamboat was the only way people had to travel. Take em right on to Georgetown—Georgetown. There bridge across the river. That for train. Old man Morris landing where used to unload the slaves. That morning that train wreck cut off all his toe. Heard train coming all the way. Old man Robertson. A preacher. Them logging trains. Come up to Romley. That the other side of Hampton. Stop track there. I used to carry lunch to them people.

Slavery times? Turn em over a barrel. Whip til blood come. That in Georgia.

Couldn't stand that. Didn't want that job anymore. Grandmother going back to Georgetown and hoe rice. "When I get back to Washington gonna be a time." Twenty-five or thirty were going to burn the house. That Hampton. Grandfather butt em with his head.

Butting head. Buttin'. Pop like a coconut. Mr. Rutledge have the Butting Room. Far side where man has a office. Neighbor bring Mr. Amos. They in the Butting Room. Mr. Amos take off long coat. My grandfather take off hat and put it on floor. Oh, Jesus. Grandfather give that man one lick and when he turn his hand loose man go on floor. Colonel Rutledge wanted to show other White people. He bet on Grandfather. Always win. I a boy.

Where people lived? Walking bridge way out to Waterhorn. Path back to where colored people live. Rutledge gave lots of land. People just scatter. They move off. When I was a boy lot more living here. "An

Army." Double houses. Still here full of people. Family on each side. Old man German kept horses for hauling logs. Mr. Brailsford had a big store. People keep houses and things clean up. Still using a broad axe to get out beams. They lay brick. Carpenter. They ring bell.

I got photos showing me, Big Washington, Big Archie on porch sitting. My family, Grandfather and all the rest. Got one a man about to step on snake. One a small white Grecian statue, woman without arms. On wall there's one of me holding a rifle. One of my father.

Johnny Garret:
Remembering the Santee Gun Club

THE TRIP TO SEE JOHNNY Garret had been circuitous and a long time coming. In the winters of 1982 and 1983, I'd worked for a few weeks culling oysters on a boat equipped with mechanical tongs. Daylight to dark with only twenty minutes for lunch. Monotonous beyond words. About ten o'clock in the morning a general stupor would set in, and with body numb the mind was allowed to wander—and since we were anchored just off Murphy Island, that was generally the direction mine would wander in. What had life been like back when?

Standing beside me at the cull table was a young Black man, William Garret. He was from the Santee community just up river. He'd been born and raised there, but in his early twenties he was a half-century too young to answer my questions. He told me then to go see his father or uncles. They had grown up on the Santee Gun Club and stayed on as guides. They could tell me about Murphy Island and the Gun Club as well. I put off going. Put off going for three years and by the time I went knocking at the office of what is now the Santee Coastal Preserve, the member of the Garret family I was looking for had been retired for six months. The assistant manager and the secretary gave me what information had been published by the state, and then urged me to talk to Johnny Garret, the unofficial historian of the place. They gave directions to his house, where his wife directed me back to the little sweet shop across from the Santee Club entrance.

I find him seated on a table nailed between two trees. A man of medium build, ageless except for a hint of white hair. A half dozen of his peers sit beside him. Yes, he is Johnny Garret. He introduces himself and says he recognizes my name. He knows my father. I don't know why this should surprise me. For the last thirty years my father has come to the Gun Club regularly as a game management consultant and as a guest hunter, too. Johnny Garret remembers him well. Would Johnny ride back through the Club and tell me a few things? He takes the final swallow from his "lunch time beer" and gets into the truck. How is my father? He is really interested. My father is recovering from a cataract operation. Johnny Garret sends his best wishes.

I suppose the first thing that strikes me is his insight. He knows not only the names and dates of club history, but also the general motivation behind who did what, when and why. Also he has a good sense of words, but not the thick Gullah pronunciation that is still familiar to this neighborhood.

"They saw Black Point pond on Murphy Island and fell in love with the whole place. It's washed away now. Black Point's just a part of the ocean." It is a far more complex story than the state's "official history" that lies on the seat between us, but then the people in the office sent me off to find him. He's relaxed. He's a guide.

Johnny says he's sixty-seven years old. Was born on the Club and raised there. His father tended the cattle and horses. When he was fifteen years old he went to work as an "extra guide" and worked at that for a good while. In those days they used sunken tank blinds. The guide stayed with the member and the "extra guide" would paddle away. That was during what he remembers as Mr. Ludie's time. When Mr. Mercer came in 1946, he went to work as a full guide. They switched over to boat blinds. The skiff was paddled up into a reed enclosure and the door closed behind. The extra guide was done away with and he was responsible for setting out the decoys and then staying until the members had shot the limit.

How long was that?

"Some stay all day," he laughs and recalls a guest who had shot three hundred shells to get two ducks. I tell him that might have been me. He can't believe that. The essence of charity. God forbid that he ever sees me shoot. Most of the members were good shots. Some excellent. And all were sportsmen. They went by the rules. Only twelve members shot at any one time, which meant between guides and extra guides, twenty four men were employed, only half that with Mr. Mercer.

By now we have driven back up the long oak-lined drive and pass the office building and guesthouse out onto the road that leads to the river And he speaks not of duck hunting, but of his early life, of work during Mr. Ludie's time and what the guides would do to earn their keep when ducks weren't being shot.

"Keeping up the dikes. Hand work. Done by task. A task was five compasses." Working that twenty-five feet of dike with a spade paid $1.50.

That was good money. As a boy he'd only been making 25¢ a day as a farm laborer and his father had cut firewood for 50¢ a cord. A cord was fifty-eight feet by four feet. You cut the tree down. Cut it up and split it and stacked it at the house, and you got 50¢ so the day's task work on the dike was pretty good. I don't doubt him, but it seems strange to hear someone speak of rice fields and tasks so long after the end of the Civil War.

We stop. To the right is a deep canal. Twenty feet across and on each side is the thick brick foundation, which is thought to have once held a waterwheel. Both David Doar and the Civil War records mention a steam mill, but all remnants of this have vanished. The water mill is all that Johnny knows of.

A few feet straight ahead of us the canal enters a marsh slue. That was the dock. A canal ran from there out to the river and up it were poled flats bringing rice from the fields on Murphy Island. The canal has filled in badly, but what once was only a narrow dike, a "cat walk," has been expanded into a road and we can follow it to the South Santee River and then turn north circling "Brick Mill" and "Deep Well," the two mainland rice fields that were planted when he was young.

What did they do with the grown rice?

They ate it and used it to bait ducks.

They were allowed to bait ducks?

Yes, they baited them with rice, cut-up sweet potatoes and corn. As the extra guide it was your job to see that these baits got on the boat, and then on the way home you spread out the bait so that the ducks would be back, two days later. No place was shot twice in a row. "Shoot Murphy one day. Cedar tomorrow." Nowadays they divided the hunting even further, into three sections.

Thick rush rises on each side but occasionally we can glimpse the canals on both interiors of the dike. To the right we were parallel to the South Santee and the delta marsh of "Embargo" rice fields. Then "Indian Hill" and "Blackwood" down river. He points these fields out. Ahead a raccoon trots in front of the truck and off into the reeds. Johnny sits forward on the seat, chuckling. "He slips off here quick didn't he?" Better fed and groomed than the coons of the salt marsh, I point out and he agrees. His interest in the animal is less academic than my own. A once and future meal, perhaps. Certainly, a hunter's interest in his surroundings. Suddenly he speaks again. And the subject is old times.

"Man, wife, children. Everybody had a bed. A bed was thirty-five feet wide and run the length of the field." I stop the truck and he points off into the distance a couple hundred yards or better. "You work that bed by hoe and axe." You worked on shares with the plantation manager. This is Mr. Ludie's time now. The manager baited ducks with his share and the worker ate his. There was something else in addition, a salary of 40¢ or 50¢ a day.

Again it is strange to be hearing this. I have seen this very field platted on a map that predated the Revolutionary War, and the contract he speaks of is just as familiar. It's a combination of the labor contracts that Ludwig Beckman had been using on Blackwood in the 1890s, contracts that I assume dated from the first days of emancipation. I can't help asking him if he didn't think that was kind of a "rough life."

He says, "No not particularly. You did what you were told back then. If you didn't then whoever told you gave you a licking and you got another licking when you got home. I toted rice from this corner here. Put it on my shoulder when I was twelve years old and toted it up there to the high ground." He points off at the distant tree line, and as the truck travels this last section of dike, he expresses his only regret. He had only a few years of school. Recently, he'd taken an adult education course in order to learn to read and write better.

We are going now to what's called the Cape—that part of the marsh which runs from the mainland east out to the waterway and south down to Ormand Hall. Ordinarily this is closed to truck traffic but at the office they gave us the okay and we set off to the right of the Rice Mill canal. And stopped almost immediately.

"I was born and raised in that patch." He points to what is now a jungle of growth. "Nothing left there, but this on the right is the guide's house." It's an ancient gray wood-sided building. "The guides slept there the night before the hunt and they ate over there in the guides' kitchen but that's gone now." Gone too are the barns and fences where his father had kept stock, but we have crossed out onto the open marsh and have entered "Mr. Mercer's time." "In '48, '49 and '50, Mr. Mercer got two men from Louisiana to come here and show them how to plant rice. They used tractors and a combine. Would empty the quarter drains good and do everything with machinery. Three years they did that."

I might have known this at one time, but I'd certainly forgotten it. For three years the Gun Club had raised rice the way it was done in Louisiana. As we drive down the center dike, Johnny points out the window on both sides. "Rice, all that rice." Only one field we passed proved too soft for the combine. In the middle of the twentieth century Blake's entire Cape plantation had been returned to rice cultivation. Johnny didn't know why, for certain, but he thought that the members had not been happy with the way operation costs had gone up following the war. They wanted the property to pay its own way. Johnny had ended up as "trunk tender" during that time. One of his father's duties had been trunk tender and he'd learned from him. He explains to me the working of the gate flaps, the notching and the time needed to raise and lower the water—an ancient art, one I would have thought long forgotten by 1948.

We drive on past fields cut by long distinct quarter drains. Bright white egrets and herons wade on both sides. We turn north and drive parallel to the waterway. He remembers the dredge *Curry Tuck* cutting through here in the mid 1930s and Alligator Creek, which had been only thirty or forty feet wide was now a wide straight shot. We are riding on dikes and islands composed of dredge fill. I ask him questions.

Indian shell middens? He knows of two on South River.

Saltwater terrapin? They were caught in the summer and held in pens for the members to eat in the winter.

Sturgeon? They sold the fish but ate the head.

My father's friend Mr. Matthiessen? Johnny was the head guide then and paddled Mr. Matthiessen. For sport he would shoot only a 4/10. Did good with it. Waited until the ducks were thirty feet in and then "powdered them."

Ricebirds? Good to eat. "Yellow as a stick of butter." Once the sky was black with them. Now a big flock was fifty.

The decline of ricebirds suggests the state of the world in general, and Johnny says that he left the Santee Club in 1942. Went in the army. "France, Italy, Sicily, Anzio. That was something." He shakes his head smiling. "Turn around in Hamburg, Germany. Came home. My parents had moved off here. I worked a year at the navy yard then went to work for Mr. Mercer as a full guide."

Does he have any regrets about coming back after the war and remaining the rest of his life here? No. He never doubted that this was what he wanted to do.

We have turned back now and head for the mainland. He speaks of Mr. Ludie's time again. And returns to the ricebirds. His boyhood, when the ricebirds would descend on the rice in its milk stage, before it hardened, "and you could squeeze the milk out into your hand." Bird minders floated along the canals cracking bullwhips to keep the birds flying. The threshing was done by hand then. "The sisters" flailed it with two five-foot poles connected by a strip of ox hide. One pole was held and the other swung against the rice and chaff "winnowed" by being blown by a hand-cranked fan. Finally you got down to clean rice.

I asked if his daddy had hunted. Yes. Ducks, deer, anything. With a muzzle loader. "A brass band," so called because its barrel was reinforced with a brass band. This would take as big a charge of powder as a man could stand to hold to his shoulder. Twenty-four deer shot could be crammed in it. Johnny had tagged along but was too young to hunt. The gun, incidentally, was gone. It would be worth something as an antique. He laughs. Someone had called last year offering him $2,000.00 for a hand-carved decoy. There had been hundreds on the place, but now all were gone.

When he was young had he gone to the salt marsh? Occasionally. He and his brother could both swim, but the creeks still made their parents nervous. They didn't go too much and never messed with oysters at all.

Mosquitoes? It's a wonder this question has been put off this long. Each time we've stopped they've poured through the windows and we've always slapped as we spoke. Were they worse than this?

Much worse. When he was a boy the only protection was a bucket with a smoldering rag and trash in it.

You put that outside the door?

"Outside the door?" He laughs out loud. You put that in the house with you and then you went through and "beat the room out with a bush they called the 'pinder windy.'" After that they started using a spray that you sucked into your mouth and blew out a nozzle.

I point out that the spray must have been poison. He points out that it probably wasn't nearly as bad as the spray that the mosquito eradication planes are dropping on us, which strikes me as probably true.

What about mosquitoes outside? When you left the cabin to go to work? Then you just did the best you could. His daddy had an ox tail with the bone removed and would slap over one shoulder, and then another, all day long.

The cattle on Murphy Island? Every Fourth of July they were hunted for the guides to be supplied with meat. Sometimes they were driven and sometimes you could just walk up on a herd. They were eating the widgeon grass, a good duck food, so the last manager, Mr. Cody—this is Mr. Cody's time—had them removed.

Boats? There were plenty of carpenters around but the ducking bateaus had been brought from Myrtle Beach. When they switched over to single guides they went to smaller lighter boats since the members were often old and the guides had to pull the boat over the dikes by themselves.

Members? Ducks? We have driven the circumference of the club and are now almost back to the shop where I picked him up. This conversation is about to end. I realize how little of it has actually dealt with ducks and members. Have I failed to ask the right questions? He has volunteered little on those subjects. Rice planting, duties of a guide and the simple mechanics of existence, those seemed to have been the topics and now it is forever too late. This dialogue is ending. His friends wait where we have left them—at the table nailed between the two trees. I shake hands and say goodbye to the guide, trunk tender and retired task worker.

Exactly a year later I went back in search of Johnny Garrett. I went first to his house but became confused and couldn't find it. I drove down to the corner where I'd left him sitting with the other men. They said I wouldn't find the house. It had burned. I wouldn't find Johnny either. He had died of a heart attack the month before.

I think what sticks with me most was left out of the interview. Lord knows why. He'd told me about the Club planting rice successfully in the late 1940s, about how they used a combine and how he'd taken on the ancient role of "trunk tender." I asked him why they stopped planting. He looked me straight in the eye and without a moment's hesitation said, "Profit margin."

Originally published in *charleston* magazine

Robert:
The Sojourner

A native of McClellanville, Alex Lofton is now retired from a Charleston bound career and living with his wife, Sarah, in a Mt. Pleasant cottage that overlooked the harbor. For a solid week I went there every night to read the letters his great-uncle Robert Lucas had written to his brother (and Alex's namesake) Alex Lucas.

"How can you do that?" my wife, Lil, would ask as I left the house each afternoon. "How can you just go into those people's house and sit there reading until after midnight?"

"Easily," was my answer.

"What if they want to go to bed?"

"I'll let myself out."

Presumptuous? Yes. But a couple of years earlier my family and I had been invited into that same house to watch films of my father, William "Bill" Baldwin and Alex's brother, Johnny Lofton, working together on their Cape Romain Loggerhead turtle project. Johnny was still in college then—just starting to work his way toward a degree in law and another in journalism. My father was just starting his yet-to-be painful career with the Fish and Wildlife Service. In the film only a few scenes included my father and the only one I recall was a beach house party. My smiling father and a smiling Johnny and a lot of girls. None were my mother. Black and white images, grainy, jumpy and authentically antique. The late 1930s were ancient history. The unknown. Alex had seen how interested I was in the Cape Romain area and the people who'd occupied it, and he was happy to share the Robert Lucas letters.

Alex hadn't read the letters himself since he was a young man, so we were entering into this adventure together. Co-conspirators in search of the past—the misplaced past. Seated at the Lofton's dining room table and provided with cake and coffee by Alex's patient wife, we unfolded and read the fading script and exchanged thoughts. From time to time, we even read aloud to each other. We enjoyed ourselves.

I won't even begin to claim this is Alex's view of his great-uncle, Robert. Of this, alone, I am guilty.

Robert: the Sojourner

The early settlers of this country imposed on the wilderness they entered a dream of old world country estates and to a remarkable degree they made this a reality. William Lucas—the youngest son of the rice mill inventor Jonathan—managed it. Two hundred and forty slaves, almost a thousand acres of rice in cultivation and his Wedge Plantation came complete with an English gate house. The Civil War changed all that—altered not only the physical reality, what children would inherit, but the nature of their dreams as well.

The next generation could look back, as many still do, at a mythical time of wealth and gracious living and inhabit the ruined land, this ghost land of their childhood, or they could dream instead of a new South, one sharing in the agricultural revolution that was sweeping the rest of the country in those post-war years. Many, like Robert Lucas, would dream both. From his father William Lucas, Robert inherited the ocean-fronted Murphy Island in 1881. And tried to sell it. Advertised as 4,232 acres of land with 650 in rice fields, he declared that the property once yielded a rice crop of 30,000 bushels. Now little is under cultivation. But cotton, corn and peas have been planted there. The island is a good range for cattle. "Eight Negro houses, tow barns, a pounding mill out of order, and a small residence on the beach in a healthy location" are included. No one is interested. And for another twenty years Robert kept Murphy Island—and for him the island would eventually become more dreamscape than landscape, more vision than real.

By 1870 dozens of the Santee Delta planters had tried to plant rice again, but the former slaves proved less than enthusiastic workers, and stiff competition was already coming from rice-growing states beyond the Mississippi and from the Far East as well. Profits were slim to none, dikes were poorly maintained and the particularly bad hurricanes of the 1890s would bring an end to the South Santee planting. The experience of the Lucas family on Murphy Island was fairly typical.

Oldest son Willie Lucas appears in the records in 1876 renting the island from the family for $500 a year. In a letter mailed from Murphy we catch a glimpse of sixty-year-old Willie. He is cooking crab cakes for breakfast. He and a friend, William Doar, are staying in the island's beach house hoping to avoid malaria while they plant what Doar's wife refers to as "the last of that wretched rice." Willie's prospects are poor and the weather stormy, but it's Doar who actually goes bankrupt that year and Willie lends him money.

Willie's younger brother Robert (our protagonist) writes from California suggesting that Willie try asparagus instead of rice since it grows enormous on the island and investors are now frightened of rice. "The Rockfish in the creeks of the island and the other parts of the river mouths," Robert advises, "are worth more than the rice crop you could raise."

We know little of Robert in the years before the Civil War. The third son, he is the only one to appear along with his father as a member of the local agricultural society and was apparently close to his father. In those years he is in charge of the family's Murphy Island holding, both the cultivation of the fields and the operation of the rice mill. Apparently the milling stands him in good stead, for during the war he serves as an engineer. And following the war he apparently returns to Murphy for a short while. Declaring that he is not able to accept the status of the newly freed slaves, he then carries his wife, two sons and a daughter off to Stockton, California, where he hopes that through hard work he can regain the fortune lost by the family. One daughter, Julia, stays behind in South Carolina.

Robert begins as a general merchant, and writes to his brother Alex that in his new surroundings it is not degrading to work at anything, "that muscle is appreciated . . . and mechanics well paid." But he is forty that year, homesick and still apprehensive. "Old trees do not bear transplanting very well," he writes and wishes himself "sitting down with Papa to a supper of cold wild duck and hot hominy."

Always the observant agriculturalist, Robert reports that wheat is the crop around Stockton and describes how one man supervises the direction of two hundred ploughs, ploughs in gangs of four and six being pulled with eight and ten horses. There was no hoeing in California and nothing applicable to the South Carolina lands. Some of his old neighbors on the delta have seriously suggested importing Chinese coolies to work the Santee fields and Robert has this advice for them: Negro labor may be the curse of the South, but the Chinese labor of California is as dear and having coolies would only help if the rice were planted "absolutely in the Chinese empire."

His career as a merchant goes poorly and by 1873 he has accumulated no capital and begins to operate a four-thousand acre "experimental" farm for others. Drought is the curse of the wheat farmer, and a canal forty miles long was about to bring irrigation to his farm. Two years before he had sold a Californian two sacks of Carolina rice seed. Now he planned to try both cotton and tobacco for his new employers.

Two years later Robert is "engaged in the strange business of making ice," for the entire city of San Francisco. By now his two sons are drawing salaries as clerks and his grown daughter (the one in California) is showing promise as an artist. Like her mother, she is "promising a life of duty and beauty." Still he is sadly disappointed. Though company supervisor, he is fifty years old and has saved no money. He can do nothing to alleviate his aging father's poverty and writes home of dreams to start his own ice business in South America or Calcutta.

Back at Murphy Island, older brother Willie has stayed with the rice and at the end of five years he is $4,000 in debt to the family—money owed for seed rice, mules and rent. Actually, Willie has not done badly, for his loses are about the same as his fellow planters, but this is little comfort to the family. Father William Lucas has now died and when the estate is settled in 1881 Robert Lucas inherits Murphy Island.

From that point on, the suggestion Robert makes in his letters to his brother, Alex, is a curious mixture of daydream and hard fact. All are motivated by an almost frantic homesickness and overpowering sense of loss. He faithfully follows the latest farming developments, reading the U.S. patent reports and even studying the weather reports for the Southern states. He advocates (with fervor) the introduction of alternate crops. Murphy Island is rich in resources. They must identify these resources and use them in a scientific manner.

Out west, wheat is growing on a desert and the ocean is yielding everything from "whales to sardines." Salmon is cheap and abundant but it can't compare to whiting. One thing is certain. Rice planting in South Carolina is over. The Negro labor was too expensive and unreliable, but then "an agrarian communist spirit pervades the world." Successful farming in the future will be that which functions with the least amount of labor. One choice is to mechanize the ten horse plows—but what Robert sees for Murphy Island is a specialization in crops and livestock, a move that will require a trained but limited number of workers and satisfy a particular and dependable market.

He's suggested sheep already and suggests them again. Cattle are suggested, too. A herd had been kept there to feed the slaves. Honeybees were a great success in California. Robert suggested one hundred to two hundred swarms for the Wedge and Murphy. Horseradishes, cayenne peppers. He suggests frogs. But even he has misgivings concerning the frogs. Frogs required little labor and sold well in New York. Still, Robert asked that Alex burn that particular letter. He did not wish to have his ideas stolen or to be accused of speculative nonsense. The estate has been settled. Murphy Island is officially his. He puts it on the market. There are no takers.

Robert places his nephew in charge of the island, but there's no hint that the young man shares his enthusiasms. Robert's instructions from California are that the rice crop at least pay the taxes on the island. Don't ask the Negro tenants for rent. Try cattle and hog raising. Hopefully the hogs won't destroy the timber. (And in the years to come the island, despite numerous other suggestions, is maintained in this way.)

In 1883 Robert suggests one hundred acres of olives on Murphy Island, though he recalls that the tree planted on the more inland Wedge never bore fruit. The next year he sends home two small packets of alfalfa seed. Alfalfa can be used to feed sheep and cattle. "I may be wrong," he writes, "but it grows in the lowlands here."

In 1885 he offers to lend money to his brother Alex who has continued to plant on the delta. And he offers Murphy Island to his brother to plant cotton on. At the beginning of that century Murphy had been used for Sea Island cotton. Alex declines. Later in the year Robert writes of a mysterious investor who might spend $10,000 to improve Murphy. No money comes and the island is rented to a Mr. Anderson to raise hogs and cattle on. Sugar pines, Robert suggests. These seeds are eaten as candy in California. Plant them in South Carolina just to see.

That is the last of the more radical solutions. If they can pay the taxes perhaps Robert "will strike it rich someday," come home and create his agricultural revolution in person. Now supervisor of the steam dredges working San Francisco Bay, he is making $200 a month, a sum his struggling rice-planting brother Alex considers princely. Robert calls it "not a salary but a slavery," for the cost of living is much higher there. What hopes he and his wife now have rest in their daughter Jane. To support her art career, they have sold their home and in the company of her mother, Jane has gone off to Paris.

In early 1887 Robert makes his first reference to duck hunters (probably market hunters) on the island. "I wish it not to be encumbered by shot gun bummers," but soon comes a reference to an agreement and an inquiry into how the duck hunter succeeds in his "pig enterprise." We have none of Alex's replies, but at this point the island has a world famous visitor.

Actually, sailor Joshua Slocum was yet to circle the world solo, so yet-to-be famous. He had lost his ship while trading in South America, and, building a giant ocean-going canoe, he was bringing his family home when he struck a whale off of Cape Romain. Entering the Santee River mouth, he left this 1887 record of Murphy Island:

"We came alongside the bank and jumped ashore, but had hardly landed when, as out of the earth a thousand dogs so it seemed, sprung up threatening to devour us all. However, a comely woman came out of the house and it was explained to the satisfaction of all, especially to a persistent cur, by a vigorous whack on the head with a cudgel, that our visit was a friendly one. Then all was again peaceful and quiet. The good man was in the field close by, but soon came home accompanied by his two stalwart sons each toting a sack of corn."

Slocum goes on to praise the generosity of his hosts, who will accept only pennies in return for provisions and the delivery of a letter. That night they all gather around the hearth and Mr. Anderson gives his version of the Murphy efforts. On this farm they had "first started in to raise pork," but found that it "didn't pay, for the pigs got wild and had to be gathered with the dogs," and by time they were "gathered and then toted, salt would hardly cure them, and they most generally tainted." Next they tilled the soil, but "the few pigs which the dogs had not gathered came in at night and rooted out all the tater." They built a fence to keep out the pigs, "but sir, the rats could get in! They took every tater out of the ground! From all that I put in, and my principal work was thar, I din't see a sprout." How or why the rats had left the crop to the pigs the year before was a mystery to him. Nevertheless, "there was corn in Egypt yet." The generous farmer said the grace and they enjoyed a meal together. "We learned a lesson of patience from this family," concluded Slocum, "and were glad that the wind had carried us thither."

Robert Lucas saw his tenants in a different light. The following year brother Alex is down with malaria and Robert, watching from the other side of the continent, saw only reports of "storms, floods and disease," for the Santee. In April the mill, long abandoned, accidentally burns. "It was there Papa and myself worked together," Robert laments. "I got there many points of mechanical information and was happy during the time I lived there, and he and I saw more of each other and were more drawn together . . . should I ever get back I will look upon the place of ashes and recall the past when all was fair and hopeful and prosperous."

The following year the island's entire profits can't pay the $25 tax bill. When Robert returns he will make it "a garden spot most productive." He does not wish to sell. His wife and daughter have inherited $20,000. But then the executor cheats them out of it. And their daughter, instead of coming home from her art studies in Paris, marries a wealthy but elderly New Yorker. "I am a little at sea," writes Robert. At year's end he offers to sell the island for $30,000 but the only offer is for 7.

In 1890 he writes to his brother of phosphate mining. While drilling a well in 1847, he'd passed through a ten-inch thick layer, which he suspects extends beneath the entire island. "At the time," he remarks, "we were all too carried away with rice culture." He suggests they drill another well. Not in hopes of mining but to trick Yankee investors into buying the place. In May his political party is defeated and he loses his job with the harbor commission. He is sixty-two years old with no savings and no job. His wife and one of his sons are sick. His lawyer leases the island for five years at $440 for unstated purposes. This is collected only twice and is Robert's only income.

Meanwhile, Alex, still farming the delta rice, is faced with bankruptcy. Robert's suggestions now center not on the island but the area surrounding.

Oysters are being planted at Cape Romain. "Should be a good thing. All depends on management." Alex should look at the lumbering going on in the upper delta. Manufacturing and sheep raising are suggested repeatedly. "I suppose you will laugh," one letter begins and then suggests that valuable pearls are found in the fresh-water clams of California. Alex should investigate those of the Santee.

It's a desperate time for Robert. His wife is going blind from cataracts. His sickly son has no job. If he had the money, he would come home to die. He tells his brother that the agriculture of the future is hard for them to even imagine. Chickens will be raised in great quantity. Asparagus will be grown under glass. Rice will be grown in boxes. All that is beyond them. It would take $30,000 to $50,000 to turn Murphy into productive pasture.

All this is certainly beyond Alex. The hurricane of 1893 has ended his rice planting. How will they even pay the taxes on the island? "The products of the earth are cheap," writes Robert. In the spring of 1895 he repeats for the last time his dream: "If I had a fortune I would open a new life to the whole coast."

And then he writes to his brother confessing the truth about his daughter Jane. They had spent a total of $7,000 on her art education in Europe. While they had scraped and saved she had studied under the best teachers, vacationed throughout the continent, attended the opera with the Rothschilds. They were told she was a great success but nothing came of it. But worst of all, what he could not tell his brother, was that his wife had objected to the daughter's marriage to the older man, and Jane, in retaliation, had stopped writing to her and eventually stopped writing to him as well. While they sat in destitution, her mother slowly going blind, the daughter had been traveling in luxury around the world with an invalid husband. One son was gone and the other sick and unemployed. Whatever financial ruin Alex faced, at least he had the comfort of a happy family and friends close by.

Though her cataracts have been removed, Robert's wife dies that November and after an absence of twenty-seven years, Robert Lucas returns—but to upstate South Carolina, for he has been taken in by his daughter Julia (a name seldom mentioned in the correspondence). And quite suddenly his life takes a turn for the better. In 1898 Yankee duck hunters lease the island and in 1900 they buy it for a hunting club. They pay Robert the goodly price of $22,500.

And so ended Robert Lucas's dream of agricultural successes, and his other dreams as well. When his dead father and brothers would come to him in his sleep, he could only bemoan the loss of a life as it had once been lived. In his final California year he had declared to brother Alex that if he could not go back to Murphy Island rich, he could at least go back there as a hermit. He could go back there to die. "I could pass the remaining years of my life on the island, and although none of the same faces would be there, I could imagine them near, when I heard the sound of the ocean and could sit under the same tree."

Instead he ended life wealthy and in the foothills of the mountains, in Spartanburg, South Carolina, and not alone, but with his daughter Julia and her family.

This essay was written in 1986. I hope Alex Lucas forgives me all the assumptions and guesswork that went into the above—I should say "presumptions." The letters were better than any historical novel, and if you're interested, they've been donated to The Charleston Museum.

Murphy Island, proper, is actually no more than a beach sand ridge, and it's hard to imagine a more unlikely spot for an agricultural revolution. The rich soil of the delta is for the most part underwater, so unless you're raising rice, you're in trouble. Still, I ought to mention the following:

In the late 1940s rice was raised successfully (if not profitably) just across the waterway. Alfalfa has been tried on the Sea Islands but with no success. The last of the "wild" cows came off of Murphy in the 1960s. Sheep were eventually kept close by on the Cape islands. The Lucases' descendents did this and so did others. The wool buyers complained they were getting "more sand than wool." The government removed them in 1935. Once the Santee River was impounded into two tremendous freshwater lakes, the rockfish fishing became a major sport—one that today probably generates more profits than the lake's small hydroelectric plant. In the 1970s dredging for Santee clams turned into a million-dollar business, but that was on the river bottom just off shore from Murphy.

Today, bees are kept on the mainland and the honey is sometimes sold. But modern beekeepers say that Murphy Island would not support bees. As you'll see in the Dick Stall piece, on the mainland, just in from Murphy Island, all sorts of endeavors will succeed.

As for the purchase by wealthy duck hunters, the story goes that the Santee Gun Club had been founded in the late 1890s by a group of Yankee (and a few Confederate) businessmen, but the hunting had been poor. Then one member happened to look over the dike into a Murphy Island pond and spotted endless ducks. A watchman ran him off, so he immediately sent someone to Charleston, leased the island for the rest of the year, and went hunting. The following year the Club paid Robert the $22,500.

A couple of years later, Ludie Beckman, who'd been leasing the last of Alex Lucas's rice fields, became the Club manager and stayed on for half a century.

Dick Stall:
Remembering

Dick Stall is seventy-three years old. He was born and raised in Awendaw, South Carolina, but spent most of his adult life at least partly away. "Partly" I say because he worked as a dredge crewman and then as a tugboat captain and so passed this way back and forth on the inland waterway. He retired not to Awendaw, itself, but to a small duck shooting place on the mainland just south of the Santee Delta. It's part of what was called the Rayburn tract. Palmetto Plantation is to the south and the Shokes Place to the north. Once the site looked out on the south end of Murphy Island, but a small pond has been built beside the salt marsh and undergrowth on its banks blocks much of the view.

Dick is the caretaker here. He lives in a trailer back from the pond's edge section of the coast. I have known him, at least to say hello to, for a good many years, and talked to him at least briefly about Awendaw and the Hell Hole Swamp area. But now I've been told that his grandmother was a German Jewess who had come to the Awendaw area to shuck oysters at Shellmore. If I ask, he'll tell me something of Shellmore Oyster Company—the tremendous operation that had once held all the oyster leases over this thirty-mile section of the coast. So I've made an appointment over the phone.

The yard is empty but soon Dick Stall arrives on a small Ford tractor followed by a beagle puppy. He wears large, plant-foreman blue work pants and matching shirt. The bottom three buttons are left unfastened to allow his belly to protrude. He's unkempt. But he's also friendly. He chews Redman. We say our hellos. Because he's hurt his foot, he stays on the tractor. From there he explains the yard. The owner encourages him to farm and on every side are the signs of successful enterprise. A large vegetable garden of several acres is planted beside the entry road just behind us. And in his yard proper are grapevines, pecans, peaches, strawberries, sweet potatoes and peanuts—and even a small patch of rice. A half-dozen chickens move about the area, under the care of a large, spirited rooster. A nanny goat is tethered nearby. Behind the trailer ducks are penned on one side and on the other a dozen ramshackle beehives stand (some obliquely) in line.

None of this, however, makes the impression on me that it should. If he hadn't taken me on a tour, most of it would have gone unrecorded, for I have my subject (oystering) and must rush to it.

Yes, he says, his grandmother on his mother's side was an immigrant brought here to shuck oysters. He computes from his own age back and figures that was at least before 1900. In McClellanville he remembers the Blacks raw-shucking oysters, but at Buckhall it was Polish women. There were other immigrants as well. He remembers English people south of Awendaw and enters a litany of occupants and inland places which have for the most part disappeared: Penny Dam, Fairlawn, Woodville, Mayrants Reserve. There were places even more remote. "Old people died in those woods," he says. "They died of malaria and typhoid."

I steer the conversation from this grim picture back toward the coast. His own daddy was a farmer first and foremost, but he'd also worked on the water. He had a forty-five-foot freight boat that was powered only by sail and pole. He was partner in another sailboat called the *Gull*. "The *Gull*'s keel is still visible, if you know where to look." With these boats they brought freight from Charleston to the Awendaw area.

But the main occupation was on the hill. His daddy planted corn and cotton, had sheep, goats, hogs and seven hundred head of cattle. He kept bees and did a little bit of everything. The Stalls were better off than many. They had a regular house to live in and they didn't go hungry. I've asked about the Cape Romain resources, and he adds that they ate bird eggs, seagull and willet and, of course, the turtle eggs. It got worse for people later on. "In the Depression," he says, "people starved. People ate stuff on the side of the road. Ate what you could run down."

By now Dick has gotten off the tractor. He limps badly, but wants to show me the closest grape arbor—"the Rayburn vine." He's transplanted it from back in the woods, from back at the Rayburn house site and centered it on a sixteen- by sixteen-foot arbor. Now in mid-prime, it is covered with tiny BB-size grape clusters. He holds a hand under several such clusters, speaking of the harvest to come. There are sixteen more vines. "Aluminum sulphate," he explains. "I split one hundred pounds between the grapevines. And the strawberries."

Next come the pecans. "You put lye around pecans. This tree was thiry-five years old, and it hadn't had a pecan on it until I got here. Now it's loaded."

And next come the beehives. These he's particularly proud of. And though the boxes are broken-down, unstable affairs, the bees appear active and many. Dick quotes the number of gallons he's taken from each. It cost him nothing to produce this honey. And he also has a long pole with a special hook that enables him to take wild honey out of trees.

Dick limps back to the front of the trailer and begins again. "You remember that big dirt cellar up by the Buck Hall cattle dip?" I tell him no. In fact, I don't even know what a dirt cellar is and so he explains. A bar of one or two layers of logs was placed in a circle around a tree or tall stump. Then beanpoles or split rails were leaned up to this center post. Straw and leaves were piled on top of this and dirt was piled on top. The radius was about twelve feet. There was just one door and no windows. He could name a good many people who lived in dirt houses. In fact, he did name them and where each was located.

I'd read about "mean dirt" houses in South Carolina in the early 1700s and seen reference to them being used again right after the Civil War, but Dick Stall was talking now about the 1920s. He repeats that these dirt cellars were common. A step up was to have a "a pole cabin," a shelter built in the more traditional log cabin way with cracks chinked with clay and gum. There were plenty of those around too when people were living all back in Hell Hole—herding cattle and doing a little patch farming.

The dirt cellar he had started telling me about wasn't back in the swamp, though. This one was right close to the Shellmore oyster shucking factory, close to the water at Buck Hall. Three women lived in it for a good many years. They were oyster shuckers. Anyway, the cattle dip pen was right close by and as boy he'd watched two old cattle herders get into a bullwhip fight there. They'd whipped each other completely bloody and he didn't know why. "That sometime lawyer, Richard Lofton," had watched the fight and at the end his only comment was "Damn fool killers." Dick was named for this lawyer.

As Dick saw it, Tuxbury Lumber Company had put an end to the cattle business in the swamp. They'd bought the Mayrant tract for seven to ten dollars an acre. There were rice field dikes all back in through Hell Hole. He'd asked his daddy how old they were and his daddy said that he'd asked his daddy the same thing. Nobody knew. They were still holding water. But Tuxbury went in with dynamite, blew them up and laid its railroad tracks (for logging trains) all through the woods. They had eight locomotives. At the camp in Awendaw they built sixty houses and forty or fifty shacks. His job with them was toting wood to "the shider." He was paid 75¢ a day for a twelve-hour day.

The coming of Tuxbury was the finish of the cattle. The sheep too. What wasn't sold off was stolen by the "new people." He thought it all had to do with politics. Banks were failing and nobody knew what was going on.

What about the liquor business during Prohibition? He answers that enough sugar was wasted to feed an army—but that was the corn liquor business. "Any old house you went to was filled with bottle liquor, sealed-up liquor, liquor in aluminum cans." This was liquor brought in from ships waiting off shore. Brought from Cuba, bottles were often sewed up in straw baskets, half-gallon and one-gallon jars. He remembers a shipload of these had sunk off Bulls Island and people got rich getting the baskets up with grappling hooks.

"It was the whiskey wars that would tear you up. They'd put the man on you." That's to say, unless a rival turned you in there wasn't much chance of getting caught. The *North Star* was a fast, yacht-type boat that had been brought from New York just for the liquor running. Dick was on a crew of men that had just finished unloading fifty ten-gallon cans of grain alcohol onto Bulls Island. And they still had some to go when they were spotted. The crew abandoned ship and swam ashore. They spent fourteen days on Bulls with nothing to eat but oysters and acorns. They stayed mostly up in the oak trees and he can remember laying on the oak limbs as the revenuers kept walking around underneath looking for them. His only other impression was that the island had the biggest sheep he'd ever seen in his life. He retired from the liquor running business after that. He'd only been along for "the fun" in the first place. He didn't see anybody keep the money they made that way. "Money made that easy—they didn't know what it was worth."

This visit was stretching well into a second hour, and Dick was growing tired. I thanked him and promised to be back when the grapes were ripe and was—almost. I went the end of August when they were just beginning to ripen. Dick had a new beagle puppy he called Baby Boy. Baby Boy had just finished chasing a rat from out of the peanuts, through the sweet potatoes, and into the grapevines where he'd ferreted it out. The rat had then run all the way back to its hole behind the shed. Dick congratulated Baby Boy. And urged me to inspect the Rayburn vine.

The vine is like nothing I'd ever seen—not even in photographs. "Burgeoning" doesn't do the vine justice. Seen from beneath the arbor, it appears to be solid scuppernong grapes with only an occasional leaf peeking through. Dick computes in his head and figures about two ounces of aluminum sulphate had gone to the square yard. The arbor is sixteen by sixteen feet. Hanging up there are what—a ton of grapes? Maybe. He says three produce people were interested. Bi-Lo stores would take them all. He will just spread sheets out underneath the vines and shake them down.

He points out an occasional dark brown grape among the clusters and we sample our way through the vineyards. At the far end is his youngest, his two-years vines. He's mulched these with dead marsh grass to keep the sun from baking the roots.

The grapes have done well, but the record heat of that summer has been hard on some of the other crops. The duck pond had suffered most, though. He points across the lawn to the diked-in enclosure. Usually the brackish water is thick with crabs, shrimp and mullet. This year the water had heated up too much and they got nothing. We turn back toward the trailer and he goes on to talk of grafting pecans and rooting more vines. Much of this he'd learned from his daddy, but he'd also worked in a nursery in Jacksonville in his time off from the dredge.

I ask about the dredge work. He didn't do much work here in the McClellanville stretch. When this was cut he was working on the government survey crew that was preparing for the purchase of the Francis Marion Forest. Besides the government dredge *Curry,* three other companies dug this section.

I ask him about captaining a tugboat. What did he tow through this section of the waterway? "Fertilizer, automobiles, oil—general towing. Anything they had." Was it a hard passage? "No. At Saltpond it would fill in. You go around at Saltpond and have to wait on tide." He'd just worked his way up to tug captain. Wasn't rough work. Twelve-hour shifts at the wheel. Twenty days on and ten days off. "I was a waterfowl," he says with a laugh. I suspect that's an occupational joke, a pun. "Stayed on the water all my life," he says.

Some of these vines aren't scuppernong. The farthest we reach has smaller, darker grapes. "A winey taste," he recommends. I eat a couple and they do have a "communion wine" taste. This vine, too, is thick with fruit. Almost as thick as the Rayburn vine. I suggest he photograph his vines. "A lot of people already have," he says.

A possum has been sneaking in at night. It won't eat the green grapes and it won't eat the skins, so far more are being destroyed than are actually being eaten. "Burn him tonight," Dick says. Just ahead is a large square rooting box. Vines are pulled down into this mixture of straw and compost. When they root they are doubled over and rooted again. "I'll pot them," Dick says. "Sell em and buy some more chewing tobacco."

We continue toward the trailer and he returns to the subjects of Hell Hole Swamp and Tuxbury Lumber and the cattle business. Politics and stealing the land and the money and who had lived where and when and finally we arrive back almost to where he'd started our conversation two months before.

"There were families up in Cotton Patch," he says. "Three or four families. They all died of malaria and typhoid and there was nobody to bury them. They were just scattered out there dead, left for the vultures to eat. I went up there years later and there's nothing to say where they lived. I had it [malaria]. Two o'clock in the afternoon start to shake—keep shaking till dark. Fever blisters on your lips. I was working on the survey crew in the '30s before I was cured. Dr. Felder cured me. My crew boss carried me into Dr. Felder, the 'nigra' doctor in McClellanville. He gave me two dozen yellow tablets. 'Adrbine.' That ended the fever."

Malaria was just a part of life. When he was growing up his whole family kept malaria. They had no screens on the house. He has a theory. "Five or six thousand years ago there were people living in North America. These were White people. They were here then and typhoid fever and malaria killed them all. Killed them off completely. The Indian came later."

I tell him that a good many historians believe that nine-tenths of the Indian population had been killed by smallpox before any White man with an interest in the matter showed up to count them. The disease brought by the very earliest of the explorers did that. Dick shakes his head emphatically and says no. Not Indians. Not smallpox. Long, long ago typhoid and malaria killed off all the White people. And then he returns to more recent times.

"Typhoid and malaria had already weakened the people. That's why so many were killed by the flu. I had a brother, a sister and an uncle all dead in seven days. People died all over the country. The flu, it was just a bad cold. I was four or five years old. I can remember watching the cow pen gap, minding the cows while my mother milked. I saw my brother and sister dead, laid out on the bed. You couldn't get a doctor. You had to hitch up and drive to Mt. Pleasant and get him and you had to have money to pay."

The story is so sad, especially when placed in context to this abundant garden setting I really can't think of much else to say or ask. We talk for a few more minutes. When he was a boy, peddlers came around and traded them second-hand clothes for eggs. After World War I there was a market for coon hides. People kept sheep. They sold the wool but they didn't know where that wool went. Dick is emphatic about that. "No wool clothes ever came back here."

I did these two interviews twenty years ago. Even at the time, I understood that from the very beginning he wanted to tell me what was important to him—the death of his neighbors and especially the death of family members during the Influenza Epidemic of 1918. Comical (and sad) that I had to stick with my prepared list of questions. Who shucked oysters? What did people eat? The story was the yard itself—what he was growing in the present should have spoken volumes about the past. At one point I was standing in this patch of ankle-high green grass and he had to explain to me that was rice.

When the interview came out, one of his compatriots assured me that I had done a great job. "The only problem is every word Dick Stall said is a lie." Well, I expect in a way you could say that about any interview. Life is a subjective experience. Don't let anybody tell you different.

Looking back, I expect the vanished race of White people were, in Dick's mind, responsible for those ancient rice field dikes, the ones that had always been back in the swamp. He carried wood to the "shider." Maybe he was saying skidder.

The phrase "watching the cow pen gap" has stayed with me through the years. These days what are four and five year olds watching?

Originally published in *charleston* magazine

The Civil War at Cape Romain: "The Blockade and Invasion of Bulls Bay"

If you're a resident of the Cape Romain area or a Civil War buff, I expect these stories will interest you, but hopefully the rest of humanity will also take pleasure in this glimpse of out-of-the-way combatants. Their frustrations and their joys strike me as universal.

Salt for the People

The members of the German artillery company were celebrating Christmas "with a little jollification." Singing carols in their native tongue, they marched by torchlight through the woods to the headquarters of the Confederate calvary unit and invited those men to share in the festivities. The invitation was accepted and, returning to their camp, the Germans formed themselves into a hollow square around a musician and two of their number who had once been circus clowns. These clowns had improvised fancy costumes for themselves, one made female by the arrangement of his blanket, and for the delight of those present, they began to dance about and work their "old jokes."

The cavalrymen, backwoodsmen for the most part, had never seen a circus before, and after peering over the shoulders of their German hosts, they would then turn about and "split their sides with laughter" when the meaning of these ribald jokes became clear to them. And the officers of the Southern calvary, watching their men, laughed at them in turn. A strange scene. A night brightened by torchlight. The sound of German voices and Southern laughter. It was Christmas 1862, and war had come to Cape Romain.

Following the general policy set by Robert E. Lee the outer islands and waterways of South Carolina had been left undefended. The lighting apparatus of both the Cape and Bulls Island lighthouses had been destroyed early in the war. There was no Confederate navy so only the Union could have benefited from their continued use.

The Cape Island was deserted. William Lucas had loaded his two hundred fifty slaves and four hundred cattle onto flats, floated them up the Santee into Wambaw Creek, unloaded and walked them through the Wambaw Swamp to a more protected plantation inland at Awendaw. On Murphy Island he left only his free mulatto miller to protect his mill property. Along the coast, beginning on the Santee at Blake's plantation and running the length of Cape Mainland, small groups of calvary pickets were stationed to observe and sound alarm if necessary. In addition a small number sometimes manned the "fort" on the northern end of Bulls Island.

The enemy for the most part was unseen or at least beyond contact. The Union blockading force with a vessel offshore of Santee and a second at Bulls Island would sometimes keep small armed boats in the Cape creeks, but they passed that way uncontested. When there was contact it was a raid of the Union forces on the mills or salt works built along the marsh edge. "A most unsatisfactory business" for the defenders who had no way of knowing when or where these nighttime raids would occur.

The headquarters for this defense was the little summer community, recently named by the Confederate forces, McClellanville. Though of dubious strategic value this village was centrally located and was relatively free from malaria. By Christmas of 1862 McClellanville's original artillery unit had been sent up to a fortification high in the South Santee. From there they could keep Union gunboats from attacking important railroad bridges. The Germans were the replacement.

Originally in command of the McClellanville artillery, six companies of infantry, and cavalry was Major Manigault. He had been busy drilling his men, erecting lookout posts and building a bridge across the town creek to unify all the elements of his command. He was popular with the local recruits, but a reorganization of the army and a new election of officers saw Manigault replaced with Byrd.

The citizens of the area had answered to man their country's call. Some were still stationed close by, but in Christmas of 1862 many were serving off, especially in Virginia. The Union blockading force was tightening its grip. Only the very old and very young had remained home. They were making do. They were making salt.

The making of salt was an ancient occupation on the Cape. The Sewee were reported trading salt in the 1500s, and it was their salt ponds at Awendaw that Governor Johnson had claimed in 1706, renaming the spot "Salthope." Still, there was no record of his success or any indications that prior to the Civil War the manufacturing of salt was a profitable enterprise here. No doubt some local consumption was satisfied, but salt making faced stiff competition. Ships sailing to England carried cotton and rice. Returning, they brought manufactured goods, a small cargo which could be rounded out with a ballast of "good coarse salt." In Virginia there were salt "works" and in the Caribbean as well. Various evaporating and boiling schemes had been carried out all along the Atlantic coast, but until the Union blockade there had been better uses for the Cape's slave labor. Now that changed.

All along the shore that faced the Cape marsh, slaves began boiling sea water in salt pots. The "pots" were actually steam boilers from the abandoned rice mills that had been cut in half and bricked about and given chimneys. Into these saltwater was placed and boiled day and night until salt was distilled. At first wooden boxes were used to hold water during low tide, but later salt ponds were dug where the water could be held to evaporate, thus concentrating its salt content. Seawater, the one asset common to all of the Cape was suddenly found to have value when placed in conjunction with abundant labor and firewood. Salt. It was quickly to become a common concern all could meet over. The slaves made it. Their owners sold it. The Confederacy was sworn to protect it. The Union swore to destroy it. An elemental substance. Confederate Private James Michael Barr only wanted to buy some. Salt, after all, had been the pay for Roman soldiers. Our word "salary" comes from this. It should have been easy for Barr but it wasn't.

James Barr was a thirty-five-year-old private in the Confederate cavalry stationed in McClellanville from May until November of 1863. His home was Leesville, a small community about one hundred fifty miles inland. There he had worked a farm with the help of half a dozen slaves, a duty that now fell on the shoulders of his wife Rebecca and several of the older relatives who remained nearby.

It's to Rebecca that James directs his correspondence from McClellanville. Fifty-eight letters over the course of seven months. His assignment is to stand picket duty. Every third day he is employed twenty-four hours staring out at the Cape marsh watching for a boat. He says this makes him lazy, this constant staring at nothing, and only once does he report to her that Yankees are sighted and a fight expected. None comes.

The McClellanville camp he describes at first sight as a "low and sickly place," an opinion he soon revises. The gnats and the mosquitoes are the only problem. They can make life unbearable, especially sleeping at night. But for the most part he becomes quite satisfied with his surroundings. The provisions are far above average. The area is a fine range for cattle and crops are abundant. "We have had bacon, potatoes, beans, squash, beef a plenty, and a few messes of venison." Another meal is "[wild] turkey, squash, cucumbers, rice, and tomatoes."

His man servant, the slave Anse, is there to care for his master. They are faring well and the letters to his wife reflect a solitary and sedentary camp life free of much dramatic incident. His pants are patched and his shoes are mended. He has a hat made. Anse almost dies from typhoid fever but recovers. There are prayer meetings in Barr's quarters and an election for lieutenant, which he loses by eleven votes. Two men die of fever. One man accidentally shoots himself in the hand and another in the toe. Five slaves escape to the Union blockade in an unlocked boat.

As for the enemy, much of what he knows he learns from the newspaper, and the only solid reminder of war he has is the sound of distant shelling going on at Charleston Harbor. The Union blockaders are said to be in the creeks but except for a single sighting, his only foray in that direction is a fishing trip made with two of the German artillerymen. "Sixty fish . . . I had a pleasant ride as I did not oar any."

His fondest hope is for a brief furlough home. He is doing his part for the war effort. He feels that many others are not. War profiteers and malingerers—many in his own community. Store owners refuse to accept his wife's Confederate money. There are some who do nothing but think of themselves while his wife with three small children is left to run the farm. He helps in the only way he can, by writing lengthy instructions on when to plant and harvest, when to butcher and what should be sold and bought. His efforts meet with little success. Without his presence the slaves don't even produce enough to feed themselves and his private's pay of forty dollars a month does not go far in the inflationary war economy. It is a frustrating situation and from his station on the edge of the Cape, there is only one direct action he can take. He can buy salt for only five dollars a bushel. In Charleston it is selling for sixteen dollars a bushel. Here is a chance to triple his money. And even more importantly, he needs to get the salt to his wife and relatives in Leesville where it can be used to preserve butchered hogs.

On his first day in McClellanville he writes to his wife of this and again two weeks later:

> *If I was at home as some are, I would take a wagon and come here after salt. I believe it would pay to haul it from here at six dollars a bushel...I wish Walter Quattlebaum could come here and look around a few days and see if he could rent some salt boilers. I think we could get them. I would like for him to boil. I would hire a hand or two and put in with him. Wood can be got at a dollar a cord. A hand could make a bushel a day or more.*

He repeats this the next week and the week after and the week after that. The salt is there and cheap but it is impossible to get it hauled. Finally, in the first week of June, he is given permission to send out seven bushels for his own use, but even the transportation of this single barrel requires a two-week wait and another two weeks in delivery to Columbia. His father is given half.

Barr wants to transport more. The price is still only six dollars, but no one will come from home with a wagon. At last, Henry (his brother?) promises to come and sixty bushels are "engaged." But no one arrives to claim it and Barr anxiously waits. Several months earlier Barr had written, "I think if our authorities give up Charleston and the sea coast that they might as well go back in the Union." Now in mid-July he has a more mundane and immediate view of the situation. If the port goes, he writes home, it will be necessary to have a two-year supply of salt laid away.

Seen from the comfortable and ration-free distance of one hudred twenty years, this linking of the salt price with the fall of Charleston seems peculiarly myopic, but Barr was hardly alone in his concern. No Charleston, no salt. On July 21, two of his Leesville neighbors arrived with a wagon and carried away fifty-three bushels, at least ten bushels of which are apparently Barr's. They were just in time for the attack of the 54th Massachusetts Black Infantry on Charleston Harbor's Morris Island. This doubles the price overnight. The following day twenty-three wagons arrive as the salt is being carried away as fast as it could be made.

Barr's interest in salt ends then. Apparently he has delivered to his wife a two-year supply and Charleston has withstood the attacks. In October, a blockade runner makes it into McClellanville. Its cargo is Turk's Island Salt. "They ask forty dollars per bushel," Barr writes. "I expect the government will take it all." Salt was the one thing they did have at the Cape and the cavalryman-farmer is clearly aware of the irony.

Local historian David Doar also mentions this Turk salt incident. As a boy he was living in McClellanville at the time and left a brief account of civilian life during the period. He recalled that the community banded together as one large family and made the best of things. There was no money for the luxuries being brought in by Charleston blockade runners. Parched rye or oats was coffee, sweetened with sorghum syrup. Flour was made from rice or corn. Old clothes were pulled from trunks or made new of homespun. And shoes made from leather they tanned themselves. They made candles and soap. For medicines and dyes they used the local herbs and for hats and baskets turned to rushes, shades and palmetto. They were content with the "plain fare as the farms afforded and especially as long as we heard that our boys were licking the foe at the front."

They had to be content, he points out, for the price of a pair of shoes had gone to forty dollars, wheat flour was two dollars to three dollars a barrel, and other food prices rose accordingly. Rice was the one thing they had cheap for it could no longer be readily disposed of on the European markets. What money there was came from the Cape's new industry, salt making. All were engaged in its making, he records, and then adds as Barr had:

> *During the Civil War a blockade runner came to McClellanville loaded with what do you think? Salt! Just the thing we did not need.*

While both Barr and Doar could see the obvious irony in the arrival of the salt-laden blockader, they would have been truly outraged to discover that the Caribbean salt could be bought for a few pennies a bushel. And though Doar complained that the "articles of contraband brought in by blockade runners were only for the rich and favored few," the articles were not necessarily luxury items. The cargo being intercepted by the Union in the Cape Romain inlets was usually salt. The ship laden with Turk Island salt was not a curious exception, it was the rule. While Barr schemed for three months trying to get home ten bushels, the blockade runners he was at least attempting to protect could be realizing a profit in salt as high as 1000 percent.

The reason for this, of course, carries us beyond the insular world of the Cape and into the subtle and complex arrangement of worldly affairs. The boiling for salt after all was not confined to the Cape shore, but was going on all along the Confederate seacoast. And the conditions prompting this enterprise were anchored firmly in the wartime economy. "Salt for the people" is how the ads sometimes read in the Charleston paper, for salt was being cut off from the common man, who like James Barr, needed it most. It was being sold instead to speculators who were hoarding it.

As early as October 1862, the Savannah paper had reported:

> *Salt begun to ascend in the speculative scale at 40.00 per sack, and hence has gone up, leaping $10 or $20 per month as public necessity varied until it has reached the very modest figure of $140.00 per sack in Atlanta. The center of speculation and the headquarters of those gentry upon whom the financial operations has been performed are plucking out their hearts to make room for deposits of gold within their iron-ribbed chests while the country is bleeding at every pore.*

A nice metaphor at the end, but the reference to gold may have been just that, metaphorical. The real damage being done by the Union blockade was that it had drained off Southern reserves of gold and silver. Blockade runners and their suppliers demanded precious metals for their services and material. With no gold to back the currency, the Confederate paper money and bonds were quickly decreasing in value and salt was becoming a reliable substitute for currency in the new barter economy. It was a convenient measure against which to gauge the value of paper, it had a utilitarian value, and did not spoil. The unscrupulous began to hoard it, leaving citizens like Barr to scramble for this necessity of life.

"Salt for the people." There is nothing in Doar's memoir or Barr's letters to suggest that the Cape salt boilers profited outrageously from this set of circumstances. The top price reached there was only twenty dollars a bushel, which could have done little more than keep pace with the general inflation. That was better than many were doing, however, and the Cape residents had their gardens, plentiful cattle and wild game as well. Life went on.

The German clowns made their ribald jokes at Christmas. On Sunday get-togethers Doar jokingly reports, "Some of the boys and girls did not attend alone for music, judging by some of the 'tête-à-tête' in the corners." And Private Barr managed to conceive a child on practically every one of his treasured furloughs home. One of these children, Charles, was so sickly, that Barr's wife Rebecca left clothes laid out for the child's burial when she went off to rescue her husband from a Confederate hospital in Virginia.

"My Dear One. May we be prepared for death at any hour for we know not the day nor the hour," Barr wrote on the November day he "bid adieu to old McClellanville." Seven months later, while engaged in heavy combat around Richmond, he was shot an inch below the kneecap. The doctor said he would heal soon and he wrote home of furlough. The wound became badly infected, and it became swollen and bruised. Flies bothered it. His hope for a furlough dimmed. Leaving out the burial clothes for her sickly infant Charles, Rebecca set out with her brother to save her husband. Twice his leg was amputated but he died four days after her arrival.

The slave manservant Anse walked from Virginia and arrived in time to help his mistress unload Barr's coffin from the train in Columbia and carry it home to Leesville. Rebecca's daughter born four months after her husband's death lived only a single day, but the sickly Charles (who did not die when his mother went off to Virginia) lived to be eighty-eight and fathered thirteen children.

The young women of a female seminary in Columbia had been entertaining Confederate soldiers about to depart for battle, and at evening's end one of them, Aletha Muldrow had sung a particularly moving rendition of "All Quiet Along the Potomac." R.V. Morrison heard her. In the first battle of Manassas he was "foolish enough to try to stop a bullet with his arm." The wound cost him the partial use of his left hand and was severe enough to release him from further service. He returned to his home of McClellanville where he began to make salt with his father, R.T. Morrison, and carry it by wagonload upstate. In Columbia he would stop to pay court to Aletha, the girl who had sung for the troops. She welcomed his attention, but fearing that she would think him a coward, he returned to service, fought in the second battle of Manassas and was wounded again. They married at the war's end and eventually had eleven sons and daughters. In the years after, Aletha would tell her children and grandchildren how her husband, before returning to Virginia, had come to the seminary in his salt wagon to say good-bye. She had seen him arrive, and even though she knew the other girls would see them, she ran down the front steps, threw her arms around him and kissed him on the lips. On every side the watching girls had clapped and cheered.

Four long years before, the Christmas celebrating members of a German artillery and a Southern calvary had done much the same.

Restless

Heard from the Southern side, the tale of the Confederate blockade is one of romantic success. Small, fast, shallow-draft schooners and larger steamers with the same attributes passed in and out of port with comparative ease, bringing to the beleaguered South much-needed supplies and carrying our cargoes of cotton, the sale of which sustained the Confederacy. Patriotism, however, was not always the primary concern of those involved. The rewards for the owner and crew were great, and one or two successful trips to and from Nassau could pay for a vessel. Adventure in the dark of night and high living ashore were the order of the day, a legend come to life in Clark Gable's portrayal of Charleston blockade runner Rhett Butler.

From the perspective of the Union, the blockade was a more sober and lackluster game of waiting. It was impossible for them to cover completely the length of the coast from Virginia to Texas. And since their opponents had speed, surprise, the cover of darkness and an intimate knowledge of the waterways on their side, it's not surprising that the Union success rate was estimated at best to be no more than one in four. Still, their persistence paid off. Gradually the Union blockaders tightened their control of the coast, and the expense of the South's evasive measures took a toll on her economy. It was still early in the war, however, when the USS *Restless*, under the command of Lieutenant Edward Conroy, was sent to patrol off the coast of Bulls Bay, South Carolina.

Though her assignments were the ocean-going vessels attempting to leave and enter the port of Charleston by way of the Bulls Island channel, the *Restless*'s captain quickly discovered an entirely different sort of traffic in the area. The old "inland passage," which Robert Mills had worked so hard to straighten and improve, was now very much in use, for schooners were busily carrying rice from the Santee River to Charleston.

From his offshore anchorage Conroy could see three to four vessels a day passing back and forth through the bay. On February 11, 1862, two contrabands (escaped slaves) came aboard the *Restless* from the *Theodore Stoney*, a fifty-four-ton schooner engaged in this inland navigation. They reported a total of twenty-five schooners and sloops similarly engaged. Still, the bay was too shallow for the Union bark. "Tantalizing," Conroy reported, and regretted that he could do nothing since he had two "common merchant ship boats" to send against them. Two days later, investigation of an abandoned sloop on the bay shoals revealed the presence of the *Stoney* and three other vessels anchored in the northwest corner of the bay. The temptation was too much. Lieutenant Conroy armed some of his crewmen and sent one of his merchant boats against the vessels at 1:30 the next morning. All four were taken that night, and Conroy hoped to salvage both boats and their total cargo of 7,500 bushels of rice. But, with no wind for sailing and the McClellanville battery close by, they had to be burned and sunk. The two owners of the *Theodore Stoney* were taken prisoner. The crew of foreigners and Blacks were set ashore for lack of space.

A week later Conroy sent the *Restless*'s two armed boats inshore of the Cape Romain lighthouse and discovered two more schooners approaching from the Santee. Hiding their boats behind Bowman's old windmill, his men surprised the first schooner, which had to be chased and fired upon. Both vessel and her departing crew were captured. They then took the second schooner, whose crew had just escaped. The larger of the two vessels drew too much water to be taken out so she was scuttled and burned. The smaller schooner and her cargo went with Conroy's men. The following day one of the armed boats was sent about five miles into the Cape Romain passage where it captured two schooners in the fifty-ton range. The crews escaped, but the first schooner was burned and sunk with its load of corn meal. The second was taken by oar past the McClellanville encampment to the Bulls Island anchorage.

It was an embarrassment of riches. Having captured eight coasting vessels in only two weeks, Conroy was now concerned that armed steamers would be sent out from Charleston to attack him. Perhaps his fears were well grounded, for judged by tonnage, at least, the vessels were as large or larger than the majority of those taking part in the more adventurous ocean-going trade. In fact, three of those previously employed in this coast's trade were soon reported carrying their cargoes of rough rice out of the mouth of the Santee River and on to Nassau. In any event, the *Restless* was forced to fall back for the moment. Reporting that she was low on fuel, water and provisions, and her deck badly leaking, she carried her loot on to Port Royal.

The U.S.S. *Onward* took her place on April 9. Moving inside the Bulls Island channel she opened fire on the Confederate fortification there and landed on the island, causing its defenders' retreat. She then anchored in the channel and waited. No expedition was sent out from Charleston to take revenge on the blockading force. But no rice schooners appeared, either. From that point on, these schooners must have taken more evasive action or carried their cargoes elsewhere, for no others were ever captured in the Cape passage.

Three weeks later, a one hundred-ton schooner out of Nassau, the *Sarah*, was spotted waiting for daylight to make an entrance, and the gunboat of the *Onward* gave chase. The *Sarah*'s crew ran her aground on Raccoon Key, set fire to the boat and escaped to the mainland. Two of the Union crew, finding liquor on board, were wounded in a brawl, and attempts to salvage her were given up. Little other activity was reported until the *Restless*, which had been cruising elsewhere, returned to the Cape Romain area in early summer.

On the morning of July 7, Lieutenant Conroy reported that from their offshore anchorage they were able to see a steamer in Bull Channel. He signaled for assistance from another nearby blockader, the *Flag*, and then knowing that low water would prevent the blockade runner from escaping farther inland, he sent his two armed boats in pursuit. On entering Bulls Bay his crewmen and those from the *Flag* discovered that the steamer, the *Emile*, was aground. At their approach the English flag was raised. Going aboard they found Captain Daniel Vincent and some of his crew still present. The cargo was reported as general merchandise. Obviously the intent of the *Emile* was to run the blockade. The Union sailors took charge, floated the ship and carried her across the bar and back into the ocean.

The Union schooner, *G.W. Blunt*, anchored at the far end of Bulls Island, did not realize the *Emile* had been taken captive and opened fire on her. On the *Emile* the Stars and Stripes were raised. The shelling stopped and the flag was lowered. The *Blunt* opened fire again. The Union flag went up again and the firing ceased. Lieutenant Conroy could report the crewmen of the *Flag* and *Restless* were in command of the prize.

Except for the minor confusion with the *Blunt*, this capture should have been due cause for celebration on the *Restless*. The blockade-running Captain Vincent had been long sought and the *Emile*, actually the steamship *Wm Seabrook*, had already enjoyed a long and prosperous career of evasion. The day after the capture the Confederates had sent a rescue party in a thirty-foot canoe. These men escaped but the crew of the *Restless* had captured the "9-oar" canoe. Unfortunately Lieutenant Conroy's first report neglected to mention several incidents of the boarding, and the capture brought a strong protest from the English government and an official naval inquiry.

On boarding, the Union sailors had hauled down the British ensign and when a passenger had made "solemn protest of this brash action" the *Flag*'s officer Lieutenant Mosman had replied, "Damn your protest; it's good for nothing." The British flag was removed and "in a passion jumped upon." No papers were asked for and with crew under guard, a search was made.

> *All Lt. Mosman's men made a general rush, during which a sailor's pistol went off, nearly shooting one of his comrades; the cabin was torn out, champagne and other liquors were taken and drunk profusely, causing intoxication and riotous conduct. The seaman's trunks were broken open and their contents scattered about and a great deal stolen; one sailor, on returning to the* Flag, *being intoxicated, fell overboard and was drowned. An officer in a quarrel with a sailor drew a knife and cut him severely in the arm.*

Unfortunate behavior, but what made the boarding a matter of such contention was the quasi-legal status of the *Emile* and many other blockade runners. Technically the ship was English and the trampling on the English flag of an English ship was bound to bring cries of indignation from the world's greatest seagoing power. Many of the crew members, as well, enjoyed the protection of the Crown, and to break into their sea chest was an outright act of robbery. The six whose collective testimony was given above all went free and only Captain Vincent and one seaman went to prison.

Since the senior officer involved was from the *Flag*, that ship took the brunt of the investigation and reprimand, but Lieutenant Conroy was forced to respond as well. It was obvious that the *Emile* was a blockade runner. The English flag had not been trampled on. Some of the men had become intoxicated but liquor had been left out purposefully by the enemy and the officers of the boarding party had thrown a great deal overboard. The seaman's trunks had been broken open not by the Union forces, but by the officers and crew of the *Emile*. The only pillage of the ship had been by the *Restless*'s crew—one pig, thirty pounds of ham and a small looking glass. There was no quarrel. A seaman had accidentally hit his head on a bayonet point. The seaman who drowned had not been drunk. Attempting to steer with a large oar, he'd been knocked overboard. Admittedly there had been irregularities and for these the only excuse that could be offered was "the inexperience of the officers and the plentiful liquor aboard."

There were no praises for Conroy and his men this time, but on September 2, the *Restless* did pick up a small sloop carrying six barrels of spirits and turpentine. A meager prize but it drew an enthusiastic response from Rear Admiral Dupont to Lieutenant Conroy. "Another of many prizes taken by your energy and vigilance."

On October 14, Conroy reported the capture of the schooner *Elmira Cornelius* as she attempted to enter Bulls Bay. At dawn she was spotted and when two cannon shots failed to stop her, the ship's boat and the *Restless*, herself, went in pursuit. Conroy's executive officer described the chase:

> *She went through the water at a furious rate, the pilot evidently well acquainted with the channel. On her reaching Bird Island Passage she*

> *entered beautifully and under full sail fairly flew through the water toward Harbor Creek. Seeing which I tried to cut her off by crossing the shoal close to the Island (Bird) but it was of no use. Suddenly, however, she took ground and by the time she floated again I was within a quarter of a mile of her; fired a rifle at her, but no notice was taken of it. She, still under all sail tried to reach the mainland; again she took the ground.*

Only then did the renegade captain raise a Union flag, upside down, in signal of distress. His distress was real for the boat was leaking badly and water was already over the cabin floor. Pumps kept her afloat, however, and the crew of the *Restless* brought out their prize.

The steward on board said they had attempted this same passage in June but the *Restless* had fired at them. For almost four months they'd laid at anchor in Port Royal Sound and then made this second attempt.

Twelve days later the steamer *Scotia* made a similar dash for Bulls Channel. Putting his two boats in pursuit, Conroy had then followed again with the *Restless* and run his quarry aground. In the course of the capture, his ship had touched bottom several times in heavy seas. "She sustained no damage, but leaks some." The *Scotia*'s captain and a male and female passenger had left the ship in an open boat. The remaining crew were "in a state of intoxication and almost unmanageable." These Conroy placed in irons aboard the *Restless* and with the help of the *Scotia*'s engineer the blockade runner was floated free. One Union seaman had drowned when one of his two ships boats swamped.

Conroy accompanied this prize to its Port Royal dockage, and in his absence the *Restless*, under its acting master, cornered another steamer, the *Anglia*, inside Bulls Channel. Conroy, returning to his ship, was aboard the *Flag* and so at last had the honor of piloting a small armed boat in pursuit. He aided in the capture and personally piloted the prize back out into the ocean. Rear Admiral DuPont's report concluded: "Before closing the dispatch I cannot forbear calling the attention of the Dept. to the energy and activity shown on all occasions by acting volunteer Lt. Conroy of the *Restless*."

Conroy next turned his attention to the land. Hearing that the mail route between Charleston and Georgetown was just inland, he sent ashore Master Mate James Russell and two "contraband" guides on the night of November 5. Once landed they met a third contraband who lead them five miles inland where they intercepted the mailman. "He at once dismounted and told me he was glad, for he had long wished an opportunity to leave the place." Carrying the mail, the party, now swelled to five, evaded the Confederate pickets and returned to the *Restless*.

This act of bravado did have a practical application for the newspapers and private letters could provide valuable intelligence for the blockading force and such items were sometimes passed from ship to ship. This particular batch proved disappointing, but their delivery was applauded nonetheless. The report on this adventure would be Conroy's final one from the *Restless*.

DuPont, in response to this matter, commented on another: "I must acknowledge your communications of ——, giving a list of vessels taken and destroyed by the *Restless* under your command, a list which sufficiently evidences the activity and energy ever exhibited by you." Soon after, Conroy was given command of the steam-powered blockade supply ship *Union*. His connection with Cape Romain had ended.

I suppose the most surprising thing about the preceding history was the almost total lack of response from the Confederate side. Most of the damage, after all, was being inflicted by two twenty-foot boats powered by five oars and armed with riflemen. When Conroy first began his attack on the rice schooners, he was warned that the Southerners had three armed boats of their own in the waterways and yet none ever appeared. A captain of the last rice schooner escaped and reported to the press that he had sailed his ship inland seeking the protection of the McClellanville battery. Yet his schooner and another were taken within a mile and a half of the Confederate fortification. Major Pinckney bragged at the ingenious uses to which the German artillerymen put the rigging and other salvage of their burned-out hull. But it was not until March of 1864 that the McClellanville battery would open fire and successfully thwart the takeover of a blockade runner. This was their first reported action and also their last.

In part, though, this record is distorted. At the war's beginning, Lee had ordered a disengagement along the Sea Islands. He did not think they could be defended and it would be a waste of resources to attempt this. There was no Southern directive to engage. But, also, there is little written record of Southern actions to consult. Though they are supposedly of both sides, the official war records are distinctly Union oriented. That was certainly true in naval matters, but on the shore the situation is little better. The official army records have brief accounts of Southern action to which we can only add the contents of a few letters, newspapers interviews and memoirs.

David Doar's description suggests a forced idleness ashore:

> *I have often heard it said of such and such a company, "Oh, they saw no fighting, they were stationed on the coast during the war." My friends, this should not be said, these men were just as courageous and devoted as those who went the storm of battle. No one knows but that they chafed under the forced inactivity.*

To these reports we can add an even fainter oral tradition from which there is no corresponding written record. Union soldiers had chased the captain of a captured blockade runner in the direction of McClellanville, but the man carrying a large amount of gold had escaped. In frustration the Union had opened fire on the village.

In the end, what we know of the Cape warfare is to a large part what the Union naval officers like Conroy want us to know, but even here we are confronted with a certain mystery. After all, Union forces continued to occupy the marshes in the years following the *Restless*'s departure and though the general policy was to patrol farther off shore with steamers, blockade runners were still using the Cape passages and some were being captured. Such adventures, however, did not occupy nearly so much of the Union navy paperwork, a fact that must lead us back to Conroy. If we examine his zealous pursuit of enemy shipping, some obvious motives are apparent. Patriotism, of course, was the first. There was also greed. The captain and crew had a small share in what they captured. Boredom was a factor, as well. The chase was a welcome relief after weeks or even months of idleness. These were the obvious but Conroy's attack on the Cape traffic appears to have offered an additional benefit.

From the very beginning Conroy was not adverse to advertising himself as well as his crew (and also the captain and crew of nearby ships), a fact amply demonstrated by the volume, content and literary quality of his official reports. And a second look at these reports shows quickly enough that for him the Cape marsh was not only a battlefield, it was an arena for personal advancement.

If he only had steam. This was an early lament of his reports but he made do with what he had. For a sailing ship to capture a steam-powered blockade runner was an amazing feat. Conroy took part in the capture of three. True, the captains of these vessels had excuses for their losses. Exploded boilers, lack of fuel and pursuit by other ships. Bulls Channel was clearly not the choice of entry for these three large ships—still they were taken. The rice schooners were taken as well as several other sail-powered ships. Rear Admiral DuPont was impressed. Those directly above Conroy were not always so gracious. They reprimanded him for risking the *Restless* and commented on his constant complaints about her condition.

But his complaints were valid and were no doubt a deciding factor in his reckless pursuit of the enemy. If the *Restless* was not seaworthy from the beginning then he had only a limited time to prove himself and work up to a more significant command. In February he complained several more times. In October he was pressing hard to abandon ship, and the following month he was assigned to the steam-powered *Union*.

The *Restless* stayed on at the Cape under the command of acting Master W.R. Browne who on December 10, personally led an ambitious raid on a salt works at Harbor Creek. Guided by a contraband, they rowed in at night with muffled oars. After becoming lost for several hours in the "labyrinth" of creeks fronting the bay, they reached the fires of the salt works at one in the morning, captured the single picket and sleeping workmen, and then demolished the boilers with axes. Returning to their boats, they were bogging out across the marsh "up to their middle in mud," when riflemen on shore opened fire. They finally reached their boats, just as forty or fifty cavalrymen came down to the edge of the marsh and began to fire where they thought the crew of the *Restless* might be. Sheltered by the marsh and creek banks, however, the men were now drifting on the ebb tide to safety, which they ensured by returning fire for a distance of some two miles.

After leading them to his owner's plantation, the slave guide disappeared into the night. None of the party was reported lost or wounded. The new captain concluded his report with, "I will here add that when I mentioned my intentions of destroying the works, all the officers and men volunteered their services."

Rear Admiral DuPont congratulated Captain Browne and his crew on their success. Two weeks later the crew of the *Restless* went ashore and blew up the Confederate fort on Bulls Island, destroying the magazine and shell rooms and burning the woodwork. It was too late for such heroics no matter how vividly recounted. A naval survey reported the *Restless* leaking too badly to be repaired in Port Royal and Browne was told to return her to the Philadelphia shipyard. He did and she was not returned to active duty.

Whether or not the blockade supply ship *Union* was exactly what he would have hoped for, Conroy (now in the Gulf) did at least have steam, and he was surprisingly successful with her. Before the war's end he captured five more steamers with the supply ship and continued to receive the praise of his commanders.

The Battle of Blakes Plantation

Captain Thomas Pinckney carried the sword of his grandfather into battle, an act that in itself implied an incalculable burden of honor, duty and obligation. His grandfather had served in the American Revolution, then had a distinguished career as statesman and ambassador, and finally, in the War of 1812, became commander in chief of all the American forces east of the Potomac.

The grandson, at thirty-eight, had no such deeds to his credit. After graduating from the state's medical college, he had lived the life of a Santee rice planter until the Ordinance of Secession was passed. Knowing the time had come for every man to serve, he had joined a cavalry company immediately. He gained what knowledge he could of tactics, and was quickly made a captain in the hastily organized company.

His first service was in guarding the coast in the Cape Romain area. This required that he keep a picket post on Bulls Island and a second on the South Santee River. The rest of his troops he kept at McClellanville. The enemy blockading along the coast would send in raiding parties against the salt works and cotton gins, and it was Pinckney's job to guard them as best he could. A service "most unsatisfactory to us" he writes, since the enemy could come and go without warning and by the time his thinly spread troops arrived, they would find only smoking ruins.

This was frustrating duty but there was an occasional adventure for he recounts in some detail the rescue of the *General Clinch*. The steamer had taken on a cargo of cotton at the railroad bridge on the Santee and had been slipping out the mouth of Alligator Creek when she ran aground on an oyster rock. After a night journey through the "tortuous" creeks, Pinckney arrived to help, but he arrived from the ocean side. Signaling, he got no reply, so approached with arms ready suspecting she was in Yankee hands. She was not. The blockade runners, seeing him come from the direction of the ocean, had assumed he was the enemy. They had doused the boat with kerosene and were about to set her afire when the cavalry captain came aboard. "Boys, he is all right," the ship captain shouted. The ship was lightened onto flats brought from nearby Blakes Plantation and the *General Clinch* slipped away to Nassau.

And so ended a successful, if brief, call to duty. Pinckney was pleased, but there was much here that foreshadowed a coming encounter—the battle at Blake's Plantation.

In 1862 a reorganization of the army brought the new election of officers. Pinckney's popular commander in McClellanville, Major Manigault, was replaced with an upstate infantryman, Major Byrd. Pinckney was not happy with this and requested that he be sent to fight in Northern Virginia. His request was denied, for it was felt that cavalry protection was necessary where he was presently stationed—an evaluation which would soon prove true.

On June 24, 1862, he recalled in his memoir five Union steamers crossed the Santee bar and proceeded up the south branch of the river. Pinckney's pickets, stationed at Blakes, reported this at once and he and his cavalry squadron galloped to the river. The steamers by then had proceeded upriver to the mouth of Six Mile Creek where at least one had run aground. Pinckney sent word upriver to the artillery Battery Warren to send down a rifled gun and he requested that Major Byrd send additional infantry and artillery from McClellanville. In the meantime, he took some of the slaves at Blakes Plantation and began to build earthworks at nearby El Dorado—fortification that would overlook the path of steamers when they tried to escape downriver.

At this point unfortunately, Pinckney recounts that Major Byrd arrived in person. He brought no artillery and ordered that the earthwork construction stop and the men be drawn away from the river. The Union steamer, meanwhile, had floated free and the fleet was returning downriver. Captain Gaillard arrived from the upriver battery with the rifled gun but only had time to send two shots after the last of the Union boats. The second shot was claimed a hit and the one hundred armed Confederate slept that night under "the venerable roof of El Dorado."

The next morning the Union gunboats returned upstream, began shelling in the direction of El Dorado, and the troops were quickly withdrawn into the woods. Meantime, downriver at Blakes Plantation the Union was putting men ashore, and Captain Pinckney, discovering this, rushed to the rescue. In a wild afternoon of skirmishes, he succeeded in killing one Union officer and saving the threshing mill and dwelling houses from being burned.

Unfortunately, the next day the enemy laid down a vigorous cannonade. They landed troops and did succeed in burning the mill, barn and houses, destroying fifty-five thousand bushels of rice and carrying off five hundred Negroes.

Pinckney put the blame for this defeat entirely on Captain Byrd. "Major Manigault or any other competent officer" would not have allowed the Yankees or their boats to escape the river. The indignant cavalryman carried his men over to Murphy Island for William Lucas's miller had suggested the Yankees might return on spring tide. They waited in ambush. The tides came and went but the enemy did not return.

This, for the most part, is Pinckney's account of the engagement. Captain Byrd's official report to army headquarters agrees on most but differs on several major points. There were four gunboats not five, and the Union steamers were each manned with twenty-one guns. A check of Union records shows this to be a great exaggeration, but it's true that the entire fleet did have at least this many guns at its disposal while he had only the one six-pounder brought down the Santee. And Byrd added, it was pointless for him to bring his German artillery from McClellanville. Despite his pleas he had never been issued ammunition for these guns. The best he could do was keep both infantry and cavalry out of the range of the steamer's guns and at the same time repulse the enemy. "I did not have a man hurt during the entire action," he concluded in a report that neglects to mention at all the destruction at Blakes Plantation or the slaves taken away.

Who was right, the cautious Byrd or the aggressive Pinckney? Could one hundred men armed with rifles and a single cannon have withstood a barrage from the Yankee steamer? Could Byrd have actually cut off the retreat of the first Yankee landing party? Could Blakes Plantation have been saved or would it have been attacked if Pinckney had not opened fire from the riverbank?

A look at the Union records suggests, if not answers, at least a more complex view of the battle. Blockaders lying at the mouth of the Santee were having some success and they were well aware that steamers like the *General Clinch* were taking a cargo inland where the trestles of the Northeastern Railroad crossed the river. It was to protect this railroad that Battery Warren had been erected on the South Santee.

On June 5, five slaves escaping from Blakes Plantation came aboard. "Capt. Blake" gave a detailed account of Cape Romain and the inland waterways as far south as Savannah. He told, as well, of the comings and goings of the recent blockade runners, and described the situation on the plantation. Mr. Blake, an Englishman, had deserted his place a week after the firing on Fort Sumter and left it in charge of a Scotsman, John McGinnis, who spent his nights sleeping inland. There were approximately three hundred slaves there. A picket guard of twenty-one cavalrymen was maintained and another three hunderd men were stationed about seven miles away.

In addition to this source, the Union had interviewed Lucas's miller on Murphy Island, and on June 12, the navy commander, Prentiss, wrote to his commander describing how Alligator Creek was being used to circumvent the blockade and suggested a blockade at this point. He also suggested that he be given a shallow draft steamer so that he could run up the Santee and destroy the railroad bridge there. "I have been furnished the names, character, and political causes of the most prominent inhabitants in this region," he writes, and asks for clear instructions regarding "their property, including Negroes." In closing he notes "a great dissatisfaction" among his men. The enlistment of some has expired already and in September all will be scheduled to return.

Prentiss received approval and on the twenty-fourth set out to destroy the railroad bridge. He crossed the bar with two large steamers, the *Western World* and *Andrew* and the smaller *Hale*. The *Western World* grounded immediately and it did not float free for two hours. The *Andrew* went aground. Finally on the night of the twenty-fifth they reached Six Mile Creek where they hoped to cross over to the North Santee. Unfortunately, the bends in the creek were so sharp that only the *Hale* could have made it and so the gunboats turned back toward the ocean.

> *Passing a second time Blake's Plantation, we were fired upon by artillery, riflemen, and cavalry. The shots passed over and near the* Andrew, *the stern most vessel. We turned back, shelled the woods, landed the marines and a party of seamen, burned the mill and dwellings that harbored them, together with 100,000 bushels of rice. Lieutenant Lowery threw out skirmished and advanced cautiously into the adjoining woods, when he was attacked by me, under the cover of the steamers. A marine was wounded in the leg and a number of others had very narrow escapes; several rebels were killed*

or badly wounded, but the accounts are conflicting. Nearly 400 slaves came down to the steamers and were taken aboard. This plantation has long been the headquarters of a regiment stationed there to protect vessels running the blockade through South Santee and Alligator Creek.

This concise report generally agrees with the accounts given by Pinckney and Byrd. Neither side, apparently, had inflicted a fatal casualty on the other. Prentiss sailed away, put his four-hundred-slave contraband ashore on nearby North Island. He returned to the North River bar, made a futile attempt to reach the railroad bridge from this direction and then went on about other business.

The attacks on Blakes, however, would have repercussions, or would have if Prentiss had not by that time sailed north. In answer to his early inquiry about property rights, the answer came back far too late. He was correct to destroy the mill and carry away slaves, but a rebel house or building should not be destroyed unless it was being used to house pickets or other military purposes—which was in fact the case at Blake's main house. Property could not be carried away from these houses under any circumstances, but Prentiss had allowed this to be done. The articles taken were assembled and shipped to Port Royal and one of the ship's paymasters was dismissed.

In the years following, such legal niceties would be overlooked. And in the final days of the war, the Union navy earned a reputation for wholesale plundering in the area. David Doar recalls, "these same men made night raids, aided by Negroes, on some of the planters' houses, carrying off all they wished—horses, cattle, poultry, household supplies, articles of value of whatever took their fancy. I went through two of these incursions as a boy, and can speak of the horrors of being waked up in the dead of night and having the house ransacked by bands of Northern vandals and Negroes."

In 1862, however, Commander Prentiss and his men were held to be accountable—but this accountability was of little use to their chief victims at Blake's, the Scottish overseer McInnis and his wife. The couple had been living there for seven years and with the flight of the owner were now in sole possession. Seeing the Union about to come ashore, they, with the aid of an aged slave, Caesar, had in the middle of the night moved Blake's fine wines into their own house, hiding the bottles between the roof sheathing and the shingles. The Yankees, learning from the other slaves that valuables were hidden somewhere in the house, hung old Caesar from a tree in the yard. He refused to talk so they cut him down and in frustration illegally burned the McInnises' house to the ground.

But the overseer had little time to mourn his unjust loss. That night or the following, he was accidentally shot and killed by a Confederate picket while walking on one of his rice field dikes. He was buried at nearby Palmetto Plantation and his wife returned in later years and erected a tombstone.

"Died defending his adopted country" was the epitaph she chose. This was true in a sense, and with one exception, McInnis was the closest thing the Cape would ever produce to a battle fatality. Confederate soldiers died of fever and Union sailors (usually drunk) often drowned. But despite countless rifle shots fired in anger or haste and numerous large shells in the direction of an enemy—despite three full years of close proximity and at least occasional bitter confrontation—there are only two official reports of mortal wounds, one to a Union forager on Bulls Island and the other to the Scotch overseer, McInnis, at Blakes Plantation.

As for Captain Charles Pinckney, his defense of his old neighborhood had come to an end. Shortly after the battle, he was moved south of Charleston to Pocataligo and in 1864 was sent north to Virginia. After three days of bitter fighting he was taken prisoner there, and since he would not surrender it, his grandfather's sword was taken from his side. Placed in a Union prison camp, his health deteriorated, and he was fortunate enough to be elected as one of the six hundred Confederate officers to be held prisoner on Morris Island in Charleston Harbor. A comparative piece of luck, for it was hoped that having the officers on Morris Island would halt the Confederate bombardment of the island.

In August 1864, Pinckney and his fellow prisoners were placed aboard the steamer freight boat *Crescent* and sent South. The conditions below deck were barely tolerable. Above deck was the Union Commander Prentiss (perhaps the same) with a guard of two hundred fifty infantry and traveling beside them a gunboat escort. The voyage was uneventful until they woke one morning to discover the *Crescent* was aground on the Cape Romain shoals and the ship was surrounded not by the ocean but by the muddy yellow waters of the Santee. The gunboat had gone on in the night unaware. Just in front of them was the Cape lighthouse and the rooftops of McClellanville were in view. The officers below quickly directed a petition to Captain Prentiss:

> *In order to save the effusion of blood, if he would deliver the ship to us we would assure him a parole and safe conduct to the Federal lines, and if not we would take the ship, as we were now* [numerically] *masters of the situations.*

Not surprisingly Captain Prentiss declined the invitation to go below and parley. He had his two hundred fifty men load their arms and fix their bayonets. Then waited. Below deck it was decided on Pinckney's recommendation that ebb tide would mark the time of attack, and they too waited for the "turning of the tide with great anxiety."

Before the tide had turned, the gunboat along with the blockader from Bulls Island arrived on the scene, and the *Crescent* traveled on without incident.

Pinckney was placed on Morris Island. The Confederate shelling continued but was well aimed and missed the prisoners. Finally his health failed to the point he was exchanged with one hundred sick and wounded and carried into Charleston.

Returning on a brief visit to McClellanville, he found the few Negroes left there engaged in making salt that was being carried upstate by wagon. He headed inland to Abbeville as Sherman advanced into the state, and when the Union invaders unexpectedly veered inland as well, he "lost two tierces" of salt in route to Abbeville. A most valuable commodity, he laments, since salt was as readily taken in exchange for purchases as gold or silver.

Contraband

In the years before the war, a slave escaping from this area was most likely to seek refuge in Charleston, where he might find work with no questions asked, or to slip back into the recesses of nearby Hell Hole Swamp. The chances of escaping the South completely by way of the Underground Railroad were slim, for the hostile boundaries of slavery reached too far beyond the Cape's edge for a trip North to be carried out or even imagined. With the coming of the war and the establishment of the blockade these boundaries suddenly shifted much closer. Slavery no longer extended to the actual shores of the Atlantic. The marshes of the Cape, if not free, were at least a no man's land to be crossed on the way to liberation.

Risking possible death, many went. But others, when freely offered the opportunity, preferred to remain. And some, having reached freedom, would then pass back and forth onto the mainland, either in the service of the Union or for personal reasons. The boundaries of slavery were mental as well as physical. The motivations of the escapees were no doubt complex, but the Union navy was quick to make use of the contraband and would rely heavily on the Cape pilots and boatmen who slipped away. The Confederates were equally quick to realize the damage these men could do. And the course of the Cape's warfare would to a large part be determined by their presence or absence.

In the first year of the war some planters had done as William Lucas and moved their slaves inland. Precautions were taken to prevent the escape of those remaining. One of Captain Thomas Pinckney's duties had been to see that no boat was left unlocked, and an owner who did so was subject to a fine. Apparently this was enforced, for when a boat did slip away, it was usually recorded as a ship's boat connected in some way with the blockade-running traffic.

On February 11, 1862, a yawl containing two escaped slaves, Harry Reed and William Maxwell, pulled alongside the *Restless*. They had been serving as crew on one of the rice schooners anchored in Bulls Bay and supplied Lieutenant Conroy with a detailed knowledge of the rebel trade including the number of vessels engaged and the depth of water in the inland passages. "Quite intelligent," Conroy reports of his new allies. But technically these men are not free. They are "contraband" property, which has been seized by the enemy.

Conroy values their assistance and keeps them aboard, but there is only limited space on the *Restless*. When his small rowed boats attack the first of the rice schooners, the crew of Negroes and foreigners are put ashore. In the second set of attacks eleven prisoners are taken. The navy lieutenant reports that five are old and decrepit slaves (one of them ninety years old and the others over sixty). Their request to be put ashore on the lighthouse island was granted. At that age, apparently, the known factor of Cape slavery and the attachment of family and friends was preferable to the unknown freedom offered by the Union navy.

The same could not be said for Blake's Plantation on the Santee Delta. Shortly after, five contrabands had slipped away from the plantation using the boat of a blockade runner and came aboard the Union *Gem of the Ocean*. The leader of this group, Captain Robert Blake, reported that he had been in the Confederate service in and around Charleston for the last nine months. His knowledge of the state's waterways was extensive and most importantly, he and the others could report quite accurately on the local blockade-running traffic, the defense of the mainland and the conditions on Blakes Plantation.

When Prentiss decided to move up the Santee River, there was little he did not know of his enemy's position, and he knew, as well, of Blakes Plantation's slave population and their plight. When owner Blake sailed back to England, he'd left behind between six hundred and seven hundred slaves, "but a great many had died from neglect and want of medicines, nearly one-half." (The 1860 census lists 535 on the plantation.) For the roughly three hundred remaining alive, there was no question of staying behind. When Prentiss landed shortly after, they hurried aboard and were ferried to the safety of North Island at the mouth of nearby Winyah Bay.

North Island offered only a relative safety, for they had traveled no more than ten miles and Prentiss had only laid claim to the island the week before. Soon Thomas Pinckney was sent to explore the inlet at the haven's northern end. If it could be forded, an attempt would be made to recapture the slaves. But Pinckney reported a channel there of ten feet, an obstacle which would be insurmountable with Union gunboats in the area. The project was abandoned.

This was to be the area's only large-scale escape, but to the south the *Restless* was still enjoying a steady supply of contraband guides—men who, having once made their way to safety, were willing to return to the mainland. The capture of the mailman requires the aid of two such guides and a third, Jack Graddock, actually leads them to the spot. Admiral DuPont, while giving out promotions, suggests advancement in the ranks for the guides as well.

Soon after, Jacob Sherman, another contraband, leads the Union attackers to his master's salt works, but does not return to the ship. He is last seen talking to a woman said to be his cousin and against orders disappeared back onto the mainland.

The Confederates are fully aware of this damage to their meager defenses.

> *A number of Negroes intimately acquainted with the networks of bays, inlets, creeks, and narrows along the coast have deserted to the enemy, and are known to have passed and repassed frequently between the fleet on the islands, and the parishes of Christ Church and St. James Santee.*

In May of 1863 a blockader reports a party of Negroes spotted on the beach of Bulls Island signaling with a white flag. Eleven in all are rescued, and though they are still referred to as contraband their legal status was changed. Lincoln's Emancipation Proclamation has freed slaves still in enemy hands, and the Union captain reports he is "carrying out the spirit of the President's proclamation." Five of the men who have no kin among the remainder are kept on the ship as crewmen—the rest, two men, three women and three children, are sent on to Port Royal.

However, the slaves escaping now are apparently not familiar with the Cape's waterways and an appeal is made that same month. "This steamer has no Bulls Bay pilot on board, and it is absolutely necessary that a steamer stationed here have one." Pilots who know the waters had been transferred out of the area and a year later a survey of the area concludes with "a colored man [Thomas Clarke] now on board the *Wabash* has been mentioned to me by the pilot in Georgetown as being conservant with the windings of the creeks about San Romain Point and Nelson Gore, last on the *Restless*, for his familiarity with the inside channels of this vicinity and that of Bulls Bay."

Neither Clarke nor Gore are on hand for the navy's invasion of Bulls Bay the following winter. Apparent victims of bureaucratic attrition, the contraband pilots had disappeared and for the final invading force the Cape was once more an unknowable labyrinth of shoals, creeks and oyster banks over which the newly arrived Black troops would make their eight-day water passage.

Lee surrendered. R.T. Morrison Jr. (my old grandpa) listed the names of one hundred twenty-three of his slaves in his plantation ledger and there in a bold hand concluded: "gone! all gone!" Soon Black troops were stationed at his wharf in McClellanville. "Astonishment" is the word usually used to describe White reaction. "Expectation" would best describe that of local Blacks. Astonishment and expectation both soon gave way to fear and anger.

David Doar wrote:

> *It is but fair to say that the Federals, who looted and taught the Negroes to loot, were only the men from the gun boats which steamed up the river... While some of the Negroes during the war went off to the enemy the majority stayed at home, faithful to the task of making provisions, serving their mistresses and doing all that could be expected of them to fulfill the trust imposed by their masters, who were away. However, as soon as the end came they, with a few notable exceptions, seemed to have lost all control over themselves and to think that all of their masters' property was theirs by right of war.*

Captain Thomas Pinckney, returning to his Santee plantation, found his former slaves refusing to work for him and were under the impression that his land was theirs. One of these, Renty, had been aboard a Yankee gunboat and met him with a uniform on and a rifle in hand and a vocal and dramatic show of defiance. Union troops were called from Charleston and the Blacks were told that though they were free the land was not theirs. Renty disappeared in the night. Hunger finally forced the others back into the rice fields, but a freshet wiped out Pinckney's first crop and he could save little more than seed for the next year. Hunger for Blacks. Despair for Whites. The Cape could still provide rice and seafood as well, but neither in successful commercial quantities. Subsistence was the order of the day and would remain the order for years to come.

The Invasion of Bulls Bay

At the war's beginning, the Union had seriously considered an invasion of Bulls Bay, but decided instead on the more southern harbor of Port Royal. A wise choice, for the capture of Port Royal gave the blockading force a far better harbor from which to operate, and in addition, the easy victory there delivered a hard psychological and economic blow to the Confederacy. Though Bulls Bay would have given them a dubious foothold on Charleston's flank, the capture of a shallow bay and the adjoining mainland would have done neither (at least not well), and as subsequent events would show, a victory in these waters was not easily won.

In the first year Bulls Island was being defended by a half dozen Confederate pickets stationed at the fort on the north end. According to tradition, this "Spanish fort" (probably a lookout built by the English in about 1706) had had its low octagonal tabby walls supplemented by a palmetto log breastwork. Whatever the case, it was not manned with vigor for the pickets would withdraw whenever Union blockaders shelled it or sent landing parties ashore.

During the summer and fall of 1862 the crew of the *Restless* had foraged on the island without incident. Foragers from the replacement ship would not fare so well, for in February of 1863 two officers were taken prisoner by fifty Confederate soldiers on a surprise visit from Sullivan's Island. The next day the large Union rescue party was ambushed and the Cape warfare claimed its second and last official casualty, Alexander Cushman, captain of the foretop.

"The impunity with which parties from the *Restless* and lately of this vessel have traversed the island has engendered an overconfidence on our part." The Union captain reported he would be far more cautious in the future. But the Confederate captain had only a limited interest in the island. Fearing that a Union launch with rifled cannon could destroy his boats, he withdrew. Conflict on Bulls Island had ceased.

On the mainland there was an equal level of inactivity. Cavalry, artillery and infantry, the approximate force of three hundred men, continued to wait and watch from McClellanville and a half dozen widely scattered picket posts. The battle of Blake's Plantation was fought, an occasional nighttime raid was made on the exposed salt works, but there was little else to occupy the troops.

In January of 1863, a confident Confederate report was filed. The chance for an attack against Charleston from the Cape area was slim. "The faculties for defense against such a movement are too numerous and conclusive." The many creeks running in from the ocean, however, offered ample opportunities for harassment and sabotage. The artillery stationed at McClellanville was "greatly inadequate to patrol the coast, but as it is all that probably can be furnished, I look only to its judicious distribution."

Judicious distribution. The dozen artillery pieces were often reported as in poor repair, without ammunition or elsewhere. The horses that pulled them were "poorly, the harnesses rotten." Already McClellanville's original unit, the Gaillard Artillery Battery, had been sent up the Santee River to Battery Warren to await an attack on the northeastern railroad bridge, an attack that would never materialize. McClellanville's German artillery had followed, being moved to a second battery even closer to the rail bridge. Now the report of January 1863 recommended that two of the four artillery pieces remaining in the village be sent to Blake's Plantation. Apparently they were not, but a section of the Gaillard Battery was moved back to the Bulls Bay shore at Andersonville. And that summer Captain Gaillard was brought down to defend McClellanville. In March of 1864 he reports the only action seen at that garrison. Twelve hundred yards offshore federal troops were seen taking the steamer *Little Ada*. Gaillard's men shelled the steamer and successfully drove off the enemy. Twenty-one shots, five hits. "The result of today's firing has convinced me that vessels entering at this place can be successfully protected by rifled guns, and I respectfully ask that the application for my rifled section at Mt. Pleasant be made again." The following week his more accurate rifled guns were returned to him.

By this time, however, the general defense of the Cape area had gradually deteriorated. By the spring of 1864, Union boats would once more be threatening the lower Santee and troops were dwindling. Stationed at McClellanville, Sergeant Philip G. Palmer wrote home to his sister living nearby. His letters help us to pick up the course of the war in the last years.

> *No company has been sent here yet, and I begin to think that none are coming. It is pretty hard on our horses and men. We are having to keep six posts but still do not complain for we are losing nothing at all in comparison with* [what] *the poor fellows in Va. and Ga. are suffering.*

His commander, Captain Gaillard, had been placed under arrest for an unnamed offense the month before and Palmer added, "The Capts. term of arrest is nearly out. We will be relieved on the 17th of June. We will be glad of it." In September, Palmer reports a lively eight or ten days, for the remaining seventy or eighty men there have been chasing escaped Union prisoners. As for their capabilities against a true attack from the enemy: "I do not see what we will do except fall back until reinforcements can be sent to us from Charleston." No attack comes but five of the men were captured while on picket duty on the Santee.

In November of 1864, Gaillard's company was moved to Mt. Pleasant, and then one section of it returned to Andersonville. Palmer writes home warning his family that they should take precautions. The enemy could land easily at Bulls Bay and march inland toward the northeastern railroad, "as there are no troops to oppose them." On December 26, Gaillard's company was judiciously returned to McClellanville and then two days later a reorganization of the army returned them to Mt. Pleasant, where it was held in reserve. Palmer reports morale is worsening. Several wealthy draftees in the company are "disheartened because the war has now come to our doors, and they are speaking in a very disloyal way."

Palmer had a more legitimate complaint to make, for in the final months of the war, he and others of his company familiar with the Cape coast are sent south of Charleston to Adam's Run, and he suspects that the artillery that has been defending Adam's Run is headed for McClellanville. He compares South Carolina to Australia's penal colony, for it "Has become as it were the Botany Bay for Generals."

Judged by Palmer's letters and the meager Confederate records, the defense of the Cape shore had dwindled almost to the vanishing point. On the Union side, however, ambitious plans were being made. In November of 1864, Rear Admiral Dahlgren had proposed a full scale invasion. Part of the troops would be landed at Bulls Bay and part would be landed in the inlet north of Charleston's Sullivan's Island. The two groups would join forces and occupy Mt. Pleasant. "This operation would require 30,000 to 50,000 good men," he writes, "because it is reasonable to admit that the present small force of rebels would receive large additions." Additions would certainly have been required on the Bay end where Palmer and seventy or eighty others waited at McClellanville and only an artillery "section" defended Andersonville.

Dahlgren's plan was not implemented, and Palmer and his company moved south to hold off the advancing army of General Sherman. Sherman had his own plans, however. He would move inland against Columbia, and if the Confederates did not abandon Charleston, he would feign an invasion to the north. Writing to Admiral Dahlgren he requested that a small force be landed at Bulls Bay to occupy the road from Mt. Pleasant to Georgetown. "This will make the enemy believe I design to turn down against Charleston and give me a good offering for Wilmington."

As a diversion, at least, Sherman's plan was to be successful, for when it came, the invasion of Bulls Bay certainly drew attention to itself. The army provided fifteen hundred men. The Union force included the deep-drafted *Shenandoah, Canandeigua, Juniata* and *Georgia*, which would wait offshore. The light-drafted *Pawnee, Sonoma, Ottawa, Winona, Potomska, Wando,* and USS *Chambers*, in addition to three armed tugs, thirty-three boats and thirteen pieces of artillery, would move inshore. After feigning a movement seaward, hopefully, the force would be able to swing down on the coast, enter the bay in the dark, and by quickly placing the army ashore, "embarrass" the enemy.

U.S. Army General Potter reported on February 12:

> *We came into Bull's Bay this morning at sunrise. I found that nothing was known about landing places or the best spots for disembarkation. The tug which brought up the topographical engineer got around yesterday and he only just arrived.*

The general made a personal survey of the area. He saw one old battery at Andersonville manned by a small force. He hoped that a safer landing could be made at Awendaw Creek and he directed that the channel there be buoyed for the "tin clad" transports. That afternoon, however, a strong northeast gale sprang up, and with heavy seas running in the shallow bay, the assault on Awendaw Creek had to be abandoned. The next morning five gunboats were sent against the battery at Andersonville, but only two small tugs could cross the bar and they could do nothing against the Confederate's two guns. The troops waiting on board the tin clads were withdrawn. The Confederate infantry force was described as "not developed."

On the next morning the gale was blowing harder. The troops were put ashore on Bulls Island for the day. The following morning another attempt at landing was made and once more the gunboats ran aground. "The great trouble has been the entire want of information with regard to the bay, its creeks and shores," the general writes. On the sixteenth he manages to get one gunboat across the bar and attacks the Andersonville defense, which now consists of four batteries and rifle trenches stretching half a mile. "The bay is a perfect labyrinth of shoals and oyster beds," the general writes, but at last the wind has shifted and the bay is calm. On the seventeenth the attack was continued at Andersonville for show and uncontested launches began to land Union troops at Awendaw's Graham Creek. Just inland Confederates were discovered constructing a new battery, but the small group manning the spot fled at the Union approach. Potter had hoped to move south against Andersonville with his whole force but the transport of the 55th Massachusetts went aground. The 32nd U.S. colored troops were sent on alone and found Andersonville abandoned.

At sunrise on the nineteenth, Potter began to march his united forces toward Mt. Pleasant. Confederate forces had retreated back across the Wando and the invading force met only Negroes coming with carts containing household goods. These turned back and accompanied the victorious army.

On the first day of the operation the Confederates had had only pickets posted ashore, and it wasn't until the third day of the assault that troops could be brought in. As Sergeant Plamer feared, these had to be rushed from Adam's Run. And even then the goal of the Union force was thought to be the railroad bridge on the Santee, not Charleston. There was even time in this lengthy assault for Jefferson Davis to be informed and to comment, quite accurately, that an attack on the railroad was far more likely to come from the Santee River, than overland from Bulls Bay.

Eight full days to land fifteen hundred troops on a shore that was practically undefended. But as victors the Union forces were in a position to congratulate themselves. "Their demonstration had hastened the fall of Charleston." "Gallantry" and "energy and endurance" were all involved, as were "courtesy, daring and ability." Only the diary of Rear Admiral Dahlgren offers a candid description of the bay's invasion. "On the first day two reconnaissances had been sent out . . . this was so well managed that by 10 o'clock these parties were aground some miles up the bay on extensive flats. Nice business." And the navy admiral is certain where the blame lies. All depended on surprise and swiftness, "but the army came without guides and no one knew where the troops were to land or how to get there through this tangled navigation."

Originally published in *Carologue*

1993 Lillian Smith Awards:
The Power of Mercy

To say I'm flattered that you have chosen me to be one of this year's winners of the Lillian Smith Award is an understatement, but to keep myself honest I must make some confessions.

Although, in my own little community, I'm still considered by some to be a wild-eyed, bomb-throwing communist, by the standards of this room I am conservative—conservative to the marrow. I can only mitigate that first confession by adding that I tend to vote the Democratic ticket. But for me voting Democrat is a form of prayer. I must tell you I am a conservative in the sense that I believe that human beings are not perfectible—for better or worse, human nature is a constant.

Furthermore and sadly, I can't claim to know much about civil rights. And I have not paid enough attention to public or even private education. I realize that these are important issues to all of you here, and I apologize.

A couple months back I watched "Eyes on the Prize" on public television and was amazed by how much I had missed out on.

During most of the sixties and half of the seventies I would wake up contemplating suicide and go to bed drunk. I could have placed Alabama on a map but not Selma. I could have picked out Vietnam but not Cambodia or Thailand. I knew that the Beatles existed but I couldn't have given you their first names.

When I graduated from high school in 1962, I was a strange little person. Dysfunctional is the word today. But back then it was strange. I had to just guess what was real. Like Brother, in my novel, I saw things and heard voices and I was attending Clemson University. At the end of the first semester they tried to kick me out. That was the same week they let the first Black man in—and that was Harvey Gantt, whom I recall was received fairly civilly. I remember his commenting on the fact he could count on South Carolinians being polite. But they weren't particularly polite to me. My advisor laughed. Said I had absolutely no future in a college, could never graduate and should join the navy.

I stayed on at Clemson out of contrariness and five years later I was finishing up a master's degree in English and teaching in an all-Black high school. I wasn't just the only White teacher, I was the first White teacher, and as far as I know, the first White person to even come through the door of that school. That was culture shock for everybody. Some of the seniors could only sign their names, but I enjoyed teaching those children and I think they enjoyed my being there. Still I wasn't in that school out of any political convictions or part of any national mandate. I was just there because I'd drifted there. And two years later I was picking oysters with an all-Black oyster crew and I was there because my wife and I had no money for food. That was 1968 and those Black men were my friends—in a way. A reverse paternalism. They looked out for me in the creek and taught me to scrap up a living. Contrary to the familiar national statistics they had families and certainly worked hard—four in the morning until nine at night, five days a week and much of that time in freezing mud and water was the norm. But of the dozen or so on that crew almost all are dead. I believe only three got shot or stabbed. The rest were killed in accidents—wrecks they didn't cause or by drowning. They died because they led hard lives and they were mortal and I suppose pieces of all of them ended up in the novel's character David Allson.

Now to return to "Eyes on the Prize." It was interesting to see Rosa Parks fighting for a seat on the bus, because in the late 1950s my grandmother's cook Anna, a tiny Black woman, had walked into the White Presbyterian church one Sunday morning and sat through an entire service. For that place and time that was an equally heroic or, at least for the Whites, an equally outrageous act. I'm sure that in 1958 there were some in the congregation who still doubted the Negroes had souls, but nobody was going to say "no" to her because, quote unquote—Anna didn't take any crap off of anybody—and because in one way or another she'd helped to raise the entire congregation or at least their children. Anna, on the other hand, must have been bored stiff by the staid Calvinism of the group. Over the last years my wife and I have gotten into the habit of attending Black church services—one or two a year for awhile. We don't go as tourists—we stay two or three hours, stay to the point where we know that Jesus Christ exists—that a tangible Christ is in our midst and life is bearable. Then, I, at least, walk out the door and this Christ dissolves. But He would have remained real for my grandmother's cook Anna, and I suspect this is the same Maum Anna who started waking me up at three in the morning a dozen years ago—a voice in my head telling Gullah stories that demanded attention—insisting that this novel get written.

So that's Anna Allson and David Allson from the novel—whom I believe are the best characters in the novel. Which brings me around to what I do believe in. And that is the spark of divinity inside of every human being. For me this belief isn't necessarily of Christian origin. I happen to be a Christian of sorts, but that is almost incidental. What I believe in is the perhaps now unfashionable notion of the indomitable and enduring. I believe that all life is sacred and honestly and truly believe that skin color, sex and sexual preference are simply veneers overlaying an equally old-fashioned concept of an all-encompassing life force. In the novel Anna Allson is the embodiment of this force. In the first draft she was the main character. And David Allson is brought on at the end of the novel to explain it all to the narrator, to show not the humanity of Christ but his outright humanness. David doesn't want to explain God's ways to man, but man's ways to God. To say this is me—that I'm willing to meet you more than half way—but I've got a right to exist.

And that's how I came to write *The Hard to Catch Mercy*. I sat down a dozen years ago determined to write about a mythical place called The Isle of Negroes—a tiny corner of the South that the free slaves would break off and run as a separate cannibal kingdom—a place where White fears, Black anger and the redemptive powers of Jesus Christ would all come together; and I did write it. But each time I rewrote, I considered scrapping the Isle of Negroes sections, thinking this material would keep the book from being published. But I didn't scrap it.

Still, when the novel was finally out and it came time to do promotion I tried never to mention race relations. Not on instruction from my publisher but because of my own timidness. I said *The Hard to Catch Mercy* was an adventure yarn—and if pressed I would say it was like Chinese boxes and had a lot of meanings. So it's a relief for me to be able to stand up here in front of you after six months of side-stepping and say that at least half of the novel is about White fears and Black anger and Christ's redeeming powers.

This was a combination that seemed strangely overlooked by everyone. Growing up after the Civil War, you did have at least two generations of Whites who felt there was a real possibility that their entire community would be massacred. Before starting the novel, I supplemented the stories I'd been hearing all my life by doing interviews, and a fairly distinct pattern was apparent—an age limit on this view. Below seventy, most Whites thought the idea silly—but they wouldn't laugh at it. I did laugh, though. Now, partly as a result of this White fear, you had incredible cruelties practiced against the Blacks. And the backlash to this is, of course, more Black anger, which I also poke fun at or, at least, let them poke fun at it themselves. Anger and humor run side by side in real life—so it is always there to pick up on. Hardest of all is to poke fun at Christ's redeeming powers, but I do that too. Make fun of and even question the fundamental reality of the entire scenario. I mock the faith that I need and want in my own life.

But I'm going to let Maum Anna Allson have the last word here. Literally the last—though she returns in the angel tales of her husband—she's last heard on earth locked in mortal combat with her life-long nemesis, the plantation master, Colonel Allson. The year is 1916. The place is a small costal village in South Carolina. A flood, with a great fire storm floating on its surface, is threatening the Allson homestead and the narrator Willie T. and Maum Anna's nephew, Sammy, have come to float the old people away in a small skiff they don't wish to share. It goes like this:

"The world dying," Maum Anna whispered when the extent of the destruction was evident.

"Put that woman off. Set her ashore!" the old man bellowed.

"I feels the cool breeze of death fanning over me." Maum Anna spoke louder. She smiled. A hot wind whipped about us, the outermost edge of the fiery hurricane drifting closer and closer to our home.

"Remove this woman!" Grandpa raised his cane and slapped it down hard on the seat between them.

"I know that old gentleman!" Maum Anna cried out. "Ask Red Willie Allson who he pa is. You ask 'em." She raised a small finger and pointed it straight at the old man, taunting him, accusing him of a crime of which she herself had declared him innocent.

"That woman is not an Allson!" the old man shouted. "She took that name just to cause me discomfort."

"Chain Anna. Chain 'em."

"That woman is not an Allson," the old man said.

But she is an Allson. A-L-L—all, S-O-N—son. Black and White, they are all the sons of God and it's God's mercy that is so difficult for them to catch—difficult, perhaps, because God's mercy is concerned not with fear and anger, but with faith and love.

The Lillian Smith Award honors those authors who, through their writing, carry on Smith's legacey of elucidating the condition of racial and social inequity and proposing a vision of justice and human understanding. I won this award in 1993 for the novel The Hard to Catch Mercy.

The State of Literature in Charleston County, November 1996

I'LL BEGIN WITH A POEM—the last you'll get from me.

Alas, for the South, her books have grown fewer.
She never was much given to literature.

For those who don't know, that's a Coolgerism—the product of a Columbia, South Carolina, printer J. Gordon Coolger. It was written some time ago and the South has experienced a couple of renaissances of the literary kind since then. But I'm afraid it's still pretty much true today. If you narrow literature down to serious essays, poetry and novels, then the books do seem to grow fewer—at least in Charleston County.

And so I'm going to talk to you about three Charleston County writers—Sam Stoney, John Bennett and Archibald Rutledge—and of course, I'm going to talk to you about myself—for in the words of the master, "I know no other subject half so well." Don't expect a true lecture. No footnotes or authoritative references. And I'm sure some of you knew these men personally and many of you probably know their work better than I do. This is a "What Sam Stoney, John Bennett and Archie Rutledge meant to me" lecture. And needless to say, I'm a fan of all three so if you hear criticism it's only the "constructive" kind. The kind we give all our deceased predecessors.

Now, I'm a self-conscious writer. While I might dash things off in the heat of the moment, I'm a true pedant when it comes to anchoring myself in traditions, most particularly the Charleston tradition. And I'm not alone. In 1984 I was in a writers' group with Jo Humphreys and Harlan Greene. Blanche Boyd was running it and Steve Hoffius was in there and Lee Robinson. And Starkey Flythe. A very heady experience for me. Intense. All of it—but I'll mention Jo and Harlan in particular because they were both about my age and like me, both had been working on first novels for many years.

I believe Jo spent five years on *Dreams of Sleep* and threw whole drafts away. Harlan wrote a thousand pages and edited down to a couple hundred for *Why We Never Danced the Charleston*. My *The Hard to Catch Mercy* was more or less finished by then—the twelve-hundred-page version that would get cut down to five hundred for its first printing. Now, all three of us felt that literature mattered and we knew Charleston literature well enough. Harlan based one of his main characters, Grimkee, on one of Charleston's stranger poets, and Mrs. Wragg from the museum was in that novel, as well. He had the feel of 1920s Charleston—the *Porgy and Bess* lyric we could call it—you can hear the rhythm in his text for the popular *Charleston: City of Memories*.

And though she'd never admit it, the same is true of Jo Humphreys. Josephine Pinckney, the 1930s writer of the Charleston Renaissance, begins her best known novel *Three O'clock Diner* like this: "Judith Redcliff floated up from the timeless and bottomless world of sleep, feeling its monstrous landscape swing away and fall before the yellow ray that pierced the eastern shutter." Jo begins *Dreams of Sleep* with: "Before they woke, sunlight is on the house, moving on the high east wall and windows through old glass wavy as broken water, onto the hard bright floor of waxed pine." And then the situation of half waking is repeated.

Now if you ask Jo about this she'll say she never read *Three O'clock Dinner* and if you press her she'll add that she never heard of Josephine Pinckney. Never the less, she's anchored in there with Harlan and me—mired in the glorious past and all its peculiar institutions—and debilitating problems—literary problems. The problems of LOCAL COLOR. The problems of the GOTHIC. The problems of PROVINCIAL LIFE AND HISTORY turned into story. The problems of GUILT.

Several years back Louis Rubin said that the Lowcountry of South Carolina could never produce any significant literature until it came to terms with its guilt. His contention (as I remember it) was that Simms and the Confederate poets and members of the Charleston Renaissance and what came after could not rise above the level of threadbare romance or local color or amateur efforts because the writers continued to insist the "darkies were happy being slaves." That may be a slight exaggeration. Rubin didn't use those exact words but I suspect that's what he meant. And I suspect for Charlestonian Rubin (Jewish and middle class) this guilt should have been felt particularly by the old aristocratic families of the peninsula who instead gloried in their ancestors' infamy.

He's right, of course. Right in the sense that you can't have modern writing without modern sensibilities. Actually, he's right plain and simple. Anyway, Harlan and Jo and I have guilt to spare. Our cups run over. But I could get in trouble claiming guilt on their behalf. Speaking for myself alone, I feel guilty about not only slavery and its aftermath, but about practically everything I do and think and feel from morning till night—and after dark, as well. That's my Calvinist heritage. My guilty genes. I'm a sinner in the hands of a very angry or at least a very unpredictable God.

And with *The Hard to Catch Mercy* (and in a less formal way with *The Fennel Family Papers*) I tried to address this guilt and to take the local color—the Gothic tradition of Charleston County—a step forward, to keep this world of the old South partially in tact but turn it on it's edge—to push the envelope. Even bust it open. Which brings me (finally) around to Sam Stoney and the others.

I never met Sam Stoney. He was an eminent architectural historian. A veteran of the war in Mexico, a famed storyteller, and fabeled commentator on the "Lowcountry Scene." Indeed, I sometimes think he invented the concept of "Low Country." He taught for years at the College of Charleston and put his stamp on many young men and women and some of these are my friends. So I've been second-handedly influenced that way—and more directly in another.

Stoney's best-known work is probably *Plantations of the Carolina Low Country*, which he did with his brother-in-law, Simmons, back in the 1930s. It's a great book—big black and white photos and handsome drawings and Stoney's inimitable descriptions of plantation life. I say "inimitable" but in 1984 I was hired to do the text for Jane Isley's *Plantations of the Low Country*. I didn't have to imitate Sam Stoney, but I did. I already knew plantations—maybe not the way he did but perhaps as well. Both my parents made their living tending and selling them and my mother had done extensive research (she still does). Plus I'd been around Ted Rosengarten for the previous five years while he was writing the plantation-oriented biography *Tombee.* In fact, Ted had read the three-hundred-page introduction out loud to me. I even had the architectural files that the IRS keeps on historic buildings, which usually include everything from ghost stories to genealogy. I had plenty of material. What I lacked was sympathy for the subject.

Those of you who know my novels (and both the published ones had already been written by this time—1984) will understand that I'm not enamored with our glorious plantation past. Slavery was an abomination. The money was blood money. But then, you could say all is money is blood money in a sense and the same fault could be found with the fine architecture of New England or anywhere else. The fact is I take pleasure in looking at houses. And most of the plantation houses around here were relatively modest. I live in such a house and make part of my living building them for other people. I guess what I truly needed was sympathy for myself. In short, to do a plantation book text I needed a persona, so I borrowed Sam Stoney's.

I went into the Historical Society and asked for Stoney's unpublished notes. Then I read those and everything he had in print straight through. Then I wrote my text, with what I hoped and do believe was a happy enough "voice." A touch of humor—an occasional hint of bemused arrogance—and an exhaustive familiarity. "I, the author, know everything there is to know about these places and I'm going to share a tiny bit of this information with you." What I needed was "Cavalier Bounce" and I got it. I only had six weeks to do the entire job and even today with the patina of hindsight, my text still strikes me (in all modesty) as not only serviceable but genuinely "well done."

We set ourselves up against our predecessors. We need to knock off somebody's hat. That's human nature and the nature of art. I have another connection with Sam Stoney.

In about 1930, Samuel Stoney and Gertrude Shelby, a woman novelist from Georgia, wrote a novel called *Po' Buckra*. The story is set in Huger on the upper Cooper River. The edge of what's appropriately called Hell Hole Swamp. (Here I'm venturing even further onto thin ice for I haven't looked at this novel in years.) A blue-blooded spinster who's maintaining a collapsing rice plantation falls in love with a man from the nearby swamp lands. They marry but unbeknownst to her he has Black blood in his veins and that tainted blood shows itself and the only resolution is to burn down the plantation house. This book is hard to find. Not a bad book. But it's dated. Anyway, it's the only novel written even close to where I live in McClellanville (about twenty miles as the crow flies) and so I went back to it often to see if I had the right feel to my historical fiction.

And I went back to it for another reason. The plot. Does that plot I just gave sound familiar to any of you? It might. Faulkner used it in *Absalom, Absalom!* A woman named Judith is to marry Charles Bon who has tainted blood and the problems of this novel are also resolved by burning down the house. Both women are named Judith. Both books have strong older Black women. In one the tainted suitor kills the brother. In the other the brother kills the tainted suitor. And both story lines arise out of a young poor buckra being turned away at the front door. Faulkner's novel was written three years after Stoney's and it's my firm (if totally unprovable) belief that he used Stoney as I did to push off on. To say, yes—but it should go like this. Which is what I was doing with *Absalom, Absalom!* as well. (At one point in the writing, *The Fennel Family Papers* began with a now unrecognizable spoof of Faulkner's opening.) And I'm not alone. I heard Padgett Powell saying last spring that *Absalom, Absalom!* was the Southern Novel—the mark that you set for yourself—though you know you'll fall far short. So I had *Po' Buckra* to move from and Faulkner to move—to stumble—toward.

On to John Bennett. I'm a fan. A big fan. John Bennett was a transplant. Ohio. Somewhere out there. He was a well-known writer of children's stories before moving to Charleston early in this century. And when first arriving he stayed for six months with the Stoney family at their Medway plantation. (Another connection. My father was manager there for thirty years.) And Bennett's *The Treasure of Peyre Gaillard* is set at Medway. A not-so-modern novel, like *Po' Buckra,* it hasn't aged well. Still, the book was interesting to me. But it was *Doctor to the Dead,* published thirty years later, that had an impact on my writing. For almost half a century Bennett had collected the grotesque legends and folk tales that were finally condensed into this thin volume. There are problems. The same theme of tainted blood and the rest of slavery's inheritance, but at least Bennett was working hard to move the genre forward—to break out of local color and rub shoulders with Poe and the French Symbolists. To stay firmly inside the Romantic tradition but to say, "Yes, but tale telling can be bent this way and this way and words can be made to do this and this." (Harlan Greene understood that and wrote a biography of Bennett that's still unpublished.) For fun I go down to the Historical Society and read Bennett's notes—and they're literally tons of them. And the unpublished novel I've got floating around now tries to duplicate what he was attempting—and of course, push it a step or two forward. The novel begins, "Now I was a sinking Peter." The sinking Peter comes from Bennett's notes. That's a fisherman without faith. Like Peter he can't walk on water so he'll probably drown. A sinking Peter. Aren't we all?

I need to hurry along to catch Archibald Rutledge. This was a man whom I did know, but just barely. He was dying in the house practically across the street from me for several years. My mother-in-law was one of his nurses. But I wouldn't visit him because I was a young snot and in rebellion against Romantic poetry and nature writing and I suppose in a sense I still am. (Except not young.) Which is no excuse. It's not just that Rutledge was a skilled craftsman—skilled enough to make a living—but he was a good person who had genuinely positive things to say about the human condition. When the complete integration of the public schools came about in the 1970s I heard of at least one high school where his books all went into the garbage. That wasn't a receptive time for the kind of paternalism he was preaching—nor today either. And my own complaint with his work would still be that like many Romantics who live a long time there's too much of it. And he's not interested in what interested me. One hunting story called "Tranquility" is set in the middle of the Santee Delta and begins something like, "As usual I spent the night with the witch doctor and his wife and in the morning hunted ducks." The rest of the story is the shooting of five or six ducks that he's already shot in at least ten other stories. And we learn nothing at all about a witch doctor and his wife who live on an island named Tranquility in the middle of a vast river delta.

But when I was writing *The Hard to Catch Mercy* I went back again and again to Archie's hunting stories and *The World around Hampton* and *Home by the River*. In *The Hard to Catch Mercy* the duck hunting chapter and the wild boar at the end, and the feel of the swamp are Rutledgeisms. And his hunting companion Will Allston was one inspiration for my character David Allson.

But as with Stoney and Bennett, too, I still approached Archibald Rutledge as someone to give a bit of comeuppance to. To push against. To say, yes but your sympathies are dated. And so are your techniques. To say life is more than this. More complicated. Sadder. Funnier. Darker. Richer. To say we must step outside of ourselves and out of Charleston County and we must wonder how we will be judged both esthetically and morally. Not too well, I suspect, for me. Maybe not at all.

I put considerable effort into writing this speech, but as I was delivering it, I began to cough. And as I went on I began to cough more and more. Toward the end it was cough, word, cough, word, and finally cough, cough, word, cough, cough, cough. I knew this hacking was totally psychosomatic in origin, but knowing that didn't change a thing. Afterward Marjory Wentworth came up and complimented me. She may have been the only person who actually followed what was being said. Anyway, in the years since we stayed pretty good friends.

Fiction

My favorite color is black. Just yesterday, a fiction editor told me that it was important for a character to have a favorite color, so that's mine. It's not a true color, of course, only a value like white and all the intermediate shades of gray, but black will do. Black heart. Black mood. Black suits, for the same well-intentioned advisor who warned me about colors also called me "a wise ass." So it's all up here right in the first paragraph. Color: black. Ass: wise. Now, let me add that I am in danger of being thirty-eight and like so many angry young men, I find that I am no longer young, only angry—angry and baffled that in spite of my best efforts to the contrary, I am still alive and for all practical purposes, prospering. There, I won't say you have the whole picture, but I think it's safe to risk an indentation.

This is a sea story. We haven't come to the boats and the water, but they'll be along soon enough. If you've seen as much of the ocean as I have and know its mind-numbing capabilities, you won't rush me. You'll be happy to read this statement of intent by the author-narrator. Note that this is neither a confession nor an apology. It is simply a clear warning that an irate consciousness is at work. I can't make of my life something that it isn't, nor can I change the way I see things. I am a wise ass. Where others find romance and adventure, I'm likely to see only the grotesque and the monotonous. The discerning reader would have recognized my bias quickly enough, so no great secret has been told, and I'm saved the useless effort of some belabored camouflage.

The remaining editorial advice I was given: Leave out the jokes, restrict yourself to five characters, and once you're on the ocean, forget about the problems of the land. Jokes? There are no jokes, only a little light- to heavy-handed irony. And by coincidence, there are only five characters. Their favorite colors are black, yellow, brown, green and burgundy. As for cutting myself off from the problems of the land, that would be impossible. Defiantly I must carry them aboard for if left behind they would have called like sirens, bikinied bathers standing on the beach waving at the trawler that slides down the side of a hot afternoon swell. It is impossible, you see, to separate the wet from the dry, the psychosis from the charm, even today from yesterday. Memory and obsession, mother and child. Ahab poked a lot of whales before he got a white one.

Now, a shrimp boat is in a constant state of decay. I guess that can be said for all the matter in the universe, but I doubt much of it can be going faster than a trawler. A twenty-year-old boat is middle-aged. At forty it's a great-granddaddy. No sooner is a new one launched than marine borers are attacking the bottom and freshwater is finding its way into the cracks of the deck, waist and cabin trim. The sea and the sun conspire to kill the paint. It festers, cracks and falls away in chips and even sheets. Spray slaps against the metal rigging. Salt slips in behind the galvanized plating and deep rust stains begin to appear wherever iron meets wood, which, of course, includes the thousands of fastenings that connect planks to ribs.

This, however, is only the obvious. Far worse is the continual stress placed on the boat by towing. And equally damaging is the melting ice in the stern bins, for here exotic fungi rush up to meet the ordinary rot that's racing from the topside down. Forward of the bins the problem is just the opposite. Operating at 160 degrees, the diesel engine and recycled fuel in the adjoining tanks bakes the interior. Paint peels away and soon the deck beams directly above the engine feather along the edges and then break off in handfuls. At our feet a stinking bilge sloshes. The engine bangs like the percussion section in the grandest orchestra. It's impossible to separate vibration from simple noise. The entire hull hums, and the blood inside our heads begins to hum along. Lordy, Lord, let's haul her out.

Now, a railway is just about what you'd expect. The boat is floated onto a cradle that's secured to railroad wheels, and these roll along an inclined track carrying the boat clear of the water. We've arrived an hour before high water. I can't speak for you, but I'm hung over. My boat is sinking. I wouldn't be here if it wasn't. On shore they're rushing frantically to get the previous haul back into the creek. Miracle. It comes off and we'll go on. The pace slows. Trance-like, the boatyard crew eases us forward with lines and long gaffs. No one hurries now. They're receiving the minimum wage. The itemized bill claims they're being paid $17.50 an hour or are worth that, which they no doubt would be if someone were delivering the extra $15 incentive into their hands. Don't complain though. An improperly chocked boat, especially an old one like this, can be badly sprung and come off leaking worse than before the pull. We're in good hands. Waving hands and suddenly, there are shouts and more shouts. The winch engages and the boat lurches forward. We must stay aboard to shift the weight by slightly lowering one or the other of the outriggers. Unfortunate, for as passengers we're deprived of the spectacle unfolding below.

I can remember as a boy a small railway operated beside my grandmother's house. The trawlers being pulled were small by today's standards—forty-five feet was about the largest—but in relationship to my size and experience in the world, they rose from the depths like monstrous amphibians whose true proportions could never have been imagined. Well over half was beneath the water—copper-painted hull, keel, wheel and rudder, all ponderously emerging. I don't know why that should have continually surprised me. If I had wanted to see the lower half of a shrimp boat, a half dozen in varying stages of disintegration were ebbed out along the creek edge.

No. It had to rise up out of the water, to float suspended in the air, and my enthusiasm was shared by many. I remember large crowds made up of both sexes and all ages attending these haul outs. They whooped. They even cheered. Small town life? An appreciation of bulk? Simple pleasures? I still enjoy watching a boat come from the water but am totally indifferent to seeing one return, a subtle sign, perhaps, that I was never at heart a true sailor.

As for my own haul out, the one we're watching only from above, well, we best abandon ship at this point. The railway operator is not happy to see me. The last time up an entire six-foot plank fell out on his caulker's head. The man told my striker to watch himself. He called the boat "a death trap." I assured the boy that the surrounding water pressure would keep all the planks in place once the boat was returned to the water. So much else was wrong, he quit a month later anyway. It was easier to find a new crewman than fix the boat.

We leave the railway and get a beer at the pizza place. Ten miles down the road we stop at the liquor store and pick up a case of Blue Nun wine. Once home we carry the twelve bottles up into the attic bedroom—more attic than room for the floors are still rough plywood, and the end wall bare siding. We crawl into the bed and begin to drink. Blue Nun, Blue Nun, Blue Nun. The time is coming when we must decide if we are going to drive our fists through the plasterboard of the ceiling or not. We've done this often in the past. Caulk-dusted pockmarks and joist right craters mar the overhead decor. It doesn't hurt. Bruised knuckles is all, but we must be careful. Our-next door neighbor hit a stud pounding this way and broke his hand. A crabber by profession, he had to hire somebody to pull his pots. Afterward, he took his family home to Virginia and got a job shucking oysters in a raw bar. He had options. We all have options. Life overflows with options and so does fiction. I promised you five characters with favorite colors, and instead, I've brought you back in time to view this sad spectacle. Myself, at age thirty, about to lean forward and vomit wine into the bed sheets.

People die everyday. Mistakes are made. Our bodies simply surrender. It can't be ice cream all the time. How often did I hear him say that? Every tow for that week we worked between the Keys and the Shoal? It seems that way in memory. Each drag sorrier than the last. Teddy's skeletal hand reaches out to toss the descending tail bag across the rail. Chaffing, multicolored, glistening, gone from sight. A flip of the wrist and the lazy line follows, slithering yellow snake, drawn back to the ocean. Crabs follow, racing to the scuppers. A diesel whine, the plunge of doors released, cables spinning, locked. Boat lurched short, steadied into another two-hour grind.

"Can't be ice cream all the time," Teddy says pushing the deck broom about the edges of the pile. He takes off his glasses and wipes the bottle-thick lenses on the last clean corner of his shirt. Wordless, he studies the ranges, then apparently satisfied, squats on the stool and begins to cull. He's not my regular crew. Teddy's a captain waiting for a boat, killing time. We both are. Basket a swing. Not really enough to tow on, but we manage to scrap up a trip. After that he gets a boat to run. Another boat and another. He goes up and down the coast until he dies.

Well, the dead only bury the dead in the Bible, and he wanted his ashes spread here, somewhere off the lighthouses. Now I'm the one coming along for the ride. A gray northeaster, a November-of-the-soul kind of day when winter is more than a promise. Cold spray surprises the deck again and again. The captain has pulled a try just for Teddy's sake. Nothing to it. Red footed, jumpy little mess that won't pay off. "Down the line." Next week they are headed down the line. The man quotes from R. Crumb: "Arr Matie, wonder what the old Cap' would be wanting with me, in this the wee hours of the morning?" The ashes are going over the stern, except for that bit blown back across our faces, and whatever it is the screaming gulls expect to get from this sudden windfall.

Gulls? Why have I brought gulls into this? Close your eyes tight reader. Don't be self-conscious. We're all friends here. I'm going to count to five. Are you ready? One, two, three, four, five. Now open them. Bright summer sunlight. It shines on blue water and white deck. Silence too. The pounding diesel has been stopped. We drift down the edge of a gently running swell. The gulls have vanished. Not a bird on the horizon. The brass urn is held high and tipped across the stern. Teddy's ashes catch and curl in the light breeze, then settle, dust the grand Atlantic, and sink.

It's been sixteen years since I had a drink, ten years since I ran a boat, and nine years since I began this story. Forty-seven years old, and now, searching like the devious cruising *Rachel*, I come upon an ending. Strange. Stranger than fiction.

Hard to believe I was ever that unhappy and hard to believe I was that unhappy for so long. Particularly sad to think that my loving wife had to endure me through all those years.

Teddy's real name was Kenny. He died of T.B. I can't say what his favorite color was. The subject never came up.

Originally published in *The State*

Terms of Endearment

WANDERING THROUGH A DISCOUNT BOOKSTORE yesterday, I was gratified to discover that Alexandra Ripley's *Scarlett*—the much celebrated sequel to *Gone with the Wind*—had been marked down. True, the book is still on the bestseller lists, but here were copies going for seven dollars below list—an ominous sign. Surely, *Starlett*'s days are numbered. Hallelujah! I didn't like the two-page excerpt in *Life* magazine. Hated it in fact. Found it laughably bad and would like to have seen every copy of the book immediately repulped. Save a tree.

And as I rocked on my heels in the book warehouse, my mind drifted back forty years, back to when there was only one Scarlett O'Hara story, and it was called *Gone with the Wind*. Everyone had read it, re-read it and stopped reading it because the movie eclipsed the book. The great Academy Award winner had been out a dozen years by then but was re-released on a regular basis. Announcements of showing dates were made with great fanfare. Discussions ensued. True pilgrimages were mounted.

Special trains would gather up passengers from rural backwaters and funnel them on to the cities where hotel and even restaurant accommodations had been booked. Richmond and Atlanta—those were the two great meccas. Sure, *Gone with the Wind* would eventually get around to Charleston and even Camden and Summerville, but it wasn't the same as riding the train with like-minded individuals and seeing the movie in an atmosphere of communal joy. I know. In 1947 and again in 1950 my parents made the *GWTW* trip to Richmond. In 1952 they saw the movie in Atlanta and what's more, they took me with them. I was only six at the time, so the train trip was a two-day blur of happy, talkative strangers and Pullman berths—but the show itself is strangely crystal clear.

"Windheads." The name sounded strange even back then. But once my parents and I had entered the semi-darkness of that great, red-velvet Atlanta auditorium, after I saw the empty seats filling with strange suddenness, seeming to grow an audience, and felt the buzzing anxiousness of these hard-core fans, I understood the term "windheads." And by extension and exceptional good fortune, I was one. "Windheads" was a label that the newspaperman H.L. Menken had pinned to us avid followers some three years earlier. He'd meant it a bit unkindly, but as is often the case, the term had become one of endearment.

And as darkness fell, the curtains parted and the crowd (already noisy) roared out. They roared continually, in fact, and would only fall silent once. But of course, this was unheard of, for during a serious drama a movie house should be no different than a church. But here all bets were off. Whistling. Stomping. And most important, shouting out lines of dialogue just ahead of the actors. Some knew the entire movie by heart, and all joined in to scream out the classic lines: "I'll never go hungry again," "I don't know nothing about birthin' no baby," and of course the unparalleled, "Frankly, my dear, I don't give a damn." This last was accompanied by such a collective turmoil that the very foundations of the building (perhaps the city) shook, and I held onto the arms of my seat tight and soaked it all in with six-year-old delight.

But the best, what I remember best anyway, was the tragic burning of Atlanta. This was the one moment when the audience fell totally quiet. It was an eerie silence that sank me back into my seat, and then only a few rows down a cigarette lighter snapped on and was held high. Then another shone in the far corner of the theater. Then others, and these were joined quickly by matches, struck and raised above heads. Dozens, hundreds, each smelling of hell's sulphur, but glowing like a sea of Dixie stars. Suddenly my father was nudging me, and bright-eyed with grand wonder, I discovered his large hand circling mine, and together we raised his flaming match. Oh yes. A grander time. Gone now. Buried under malls and discount bookstores. A child's memory. Gone with the wind.

Note 2004: Please don't write me any notes or call me telling me how lucky I was to experience something like this. The entire piece is a joke. A "Dead Head" is a hard-core Greatful Dead fan and borrowing from that, a "Parrot Head" is a hard-core Jimmy Buffett fan. I did attend a Jimmy Buffett concert thirty years ago, but the theater description used here is based on what I've read about showings of the black-hearted cult classic The Rocky Horror Picture Show. *Trust me this did not happen in Atlanta in 1952. At least I don't think so. If it did, I wasn't there and neither were my parents—though recently my mother did say she hadn't been to a movie theater in fifty years. She said the last movie she went to was* Gone with the Wind.

Originally published in *charleston* magazine

Possessions

This essay appeared along with those of five other writers in Picturing the South: 1860 to the Present. *It was reprinted several times. By chopping off the end,* Veranda *made it into a funny piece about antique collecting.*

In 1952 or thereabouts, our family was living in the small town of Bluffton, South Carolina. We had put Savannah behind us—twenty miles behind us. My father, a U.S. Fish and Wildlife biologist, still drove to the city to work, but we were out of the cracker box duplex in the treeless "Oakwood" subdivision. We had a home of our own. Small but new, and on the salt marsh with great moss-spangled live oaks on every side. I was eight years old and my mother became a partner in an antiques shop. And she took me on as an assistant . . . of sorts.

The new house had been a wild extravagance and left no money for purchasing antiques, so my mother and her cousin Anne searched the Salvation Army and Goodwill stores in Savannah for misplaced heirlooms. A bedraggled china-headed doll bought for a dime sold for eighty dollars. Some battered tin plates turned out to be pewter. A pewter mug turned out to be a silver cup made in London two centuries earlier. My mother kept that. There was magic in old things.

My mother and her cousin Anne would load us children (six in all) in the back of Anne's station wagon and take the ferry to Hilton Head Island. Only two White families on the island that I recall and three or four automobiles. Black men straddled marsh tacky ponies. The bare feet of these men brushed the ground. Orange trees growing wild. A semi-lost world.

But we hadn't come as tourists. We children were driven to old Fort Walker on the north end of the island and put to work combing the concrete ruins, the beach and the adjoining creek banks. We filled bushel baskets with cannon balls, musket balls, wine bottles, china and even coins. Some of this was Spanish-American War debris. Most dated from the Civil War.

In November of 1861, a Union fleet of seventy-seven vessels had sailed into view. On neighboring St. Helena Island the local militia got drunk and had a lancing tournament in preparation for battle, but here on Hilton Head a thousand grim-faced reinforcements dug in to defend Walker's artillery batteries. To no avail. The Northern fleet represented the largest concentration of firepower ever known since the beginning of time, and in a matter of hours strategic Port Royal Sound was lost and Hilton Head was abandoned. The plantation owners escaped to Bluffton. Then, realizing that their mansions would give comfort to the enemy, the most zealous slipped back to the island and burned down their own homes—and those of their neighbors as well. Such buffoonery. Such lethal buffoonery. By April of 1865 it had killed six hundred thousand men.

On the mainland trips I would go alone with my mother. She would drive into the Black neighborhoods ten miles away. Twenty miles away. Fifty miles away. She was a small woman. She would slide over against the driver's-side door and prop me, an eight-year old, behind the steering wheel of the slowly moving automobile. Then she would extend herself half out of the window but somehow manage to keep her toe on the accelerator.

"You got any old things?" That's what she shouted at the Black inhabitants. Then back at me she'd shout, "Stay on the road!" Then back out the window: "You got any old things?"

They did. Black women with wizened or cherubic faces and all with kerchiefed heads waved her over and led us past the scrap-lumber shanties and into their backyard sheds. Antebellum furniture. Bottomless three-legged chairs. Broken-back lowboys. Chicken droppings on top and the legs eaten away by termites. Most of these things were bought for next to nothing, washed off, patched up and sold for a few dollars more.

"When the big houses burned, they carried this furniture out." That was my mother's explanation, and one that made sense . . . sort of. She didn't bother to add that she and I were systematically following the path of Sherman's March. Sherman, as the old joke goes, said "War is Hell!" and set out to prove it. He burned Atlanta, marched to the sea, bivouacked in an unharmed Savannah for Christmas in 1865, and headed off for Columbia. Once in South Carolina, his men burned practically everything they came to. White residents fled and the freed slaves emptied the houses of furniture before they were lit. And eighty-five years later a White woman came by shouting "You got any old things?" An eight-year -old boy was driving the car.

Actually, it took me another forty years to figure this out. I was working on a tour guidebook and traveling those same roads with my aging father. Since leaving the government in 1955, he'd been working with modern-day plantation owners as a wildlife consultant and selling plantations as well. He knew poor old Jasper County like the back of his Wilmington, Delaware, carpetbagging hand. He muttered, "Sherman, that bastard." We stayed in a motel. He sat up in the middle of the night, looked straight at me, and said, "The plantation. You understand. The place." He was still sound asleep. I said "Yes," which was only a partial lie, and he lay down.

I'm a sucker for old photographs. Once I bought a second-hand copy stand and tried to copy every family album in the vicinity. Another time I rode the train to Washington, D.C., to look at the "Southern" WPA photographs in the Library of Congress. It took three and a half days of steady flipping.

Every picture tells a story. That's oh so true. One in *Picturing the South* is labeled "Hamilton, a Slave at the Legare Plantation, Capers Island, South Carolina." A man is shown climbing into a carriage. A house in the background with women occupants. A second man holds the horse steady. I assume the humble horse-holder is "Hamilton, a Slave."

Now, the census records of 1820 put my great-great-great grandfather on Capers Island. He married one of the Legare daughters and they went to the Indian frontier of Alabama. She went insane and died. He came back with his family to McClellanville, South Carolina, which is where I live today—which is where I sit studying the picture of Hamilton the slave and reflecting on the fact that my mother's people owned this man.

Originally published in *Picturing the South: 1860 to the Present*

Good Morning America

A YEAR AFTER HURRICANE HUGO, the *Good Morning America* helicopter made several passes over the creek in preparation for the "one year anniversary of Hurricane Hugo" programming that was aired in September. Two of my shrimping relatives went in the ocean instead of participating in the ground-based interviews filmed in advance. Surely a good sign. The media harvest is winding down. The harvest of the sea triumphs.

Hooray and a sigh. Fifteen months ago my wife and I picked our way among the fallen trees that blocked these streets. On every side, mud, marsh grass and dead fish were mixed with parts of houses and house parts. An entire fleet of shrimp boats had been flung high and dry upon what was once "the hill." Helicopters hovered overhead that day as well, taking television photos that I suppose were shown that night or the next. We had no way of knowing, for electricity wouldn't return for another three weeks. And I assumed we got the usual ten-second "bite," but judging by what happened next there must have been much, much more. Huddling over a battery-operated radio that night, I heard the South Carolina governor declare that "the town of McClellanville no longer exists." "Reports of my death were greatly exaggerated," quipped Twain. The governor must have retracted soon after—and with a vengeance—for in the days that followed I would come to think "reports of our existence were greatly exaggerated."

True, I wasn't happy to hear our obituary. Especially since at least a hundred citizens of the town proper and thousands in the inundated area had miraculously survived a tidal surge of sixteen feet and hurricane winds that probably exceeded 175 miles per hour. Many of us that morning had been wandering through the rubble being photographed. We weren't dead, just in shock and hardly prepared for the thirty-eight trailer trucks of relief supplies that arrived one night. Suddenly, there was an army of well-meaning help swelling our tiny community of four hundred souls. President Bush even tried to squeeze in but was rerouted at the last minute down to Charleston. Bad weather was the official reason given but a false report to the Secret Service of dead bodies and rifles was the rumor. Rumors. There were lots of rumors and chaos that would rival the most surreal of Fellini's carnivals.

Despair, greed and petty corruption. That's what the cynic in me recalls most. What lobe of the brain is that? Perhaps the rear-reptilian. Shame on me, for now almost one year later the town is at least recognizable. The large pines are gone but the great sprawling live oaks have survived. Homes have been repaired and new ones are being built. The shrimp boats are not leaning against houses but in the ocean towing. Dogs, church, children—what we expect of normalcy, all are there in record time.

Without the federal disaster aid (delivered by sometimes generous, always bumbling bureaucrats), without the Marines (now I understand the concept of marital law), without the Corps of Engineers (the S.O.B.'s finally found a job big enough to suit them and they were very, very good at it), without the Red Cross (they tried) and without the insurance adjusters (your life is in the palm of their tightly gripped fists), without all these the rebuilding of the town would have dragged on for decades. Without the churches (God does exist—watch a Mennonite hammer), without all the volunteers (such astounding generosity from every corner of the county), without the cash donations and the truckloads of food, clothing and building material, and without the media (they've got to be included), without all these it's possible our little community would never been rebuilt.

So why now, with the *Good Morning America* helicopter chopping off over the slightly crippled horizon, why do I feel such anger toward my fellow man and most of all toward myself? I'm not alone. Tempers still flare. Depression and insomnia are the norm. The subject of Hugo Stress drifts through every conversation. It's not psychobabble if it's happening to you or your friends and neighbors. Obviously, all this anger has something to do with loss. We have our town back, but it's not "Our town." I'm guessing that the words that apply are the optimism of innocence. Maybe we lost it at the movies. Or maybe we just lost it.

While I was entering this piece into the computer, Hurricane Charlie crossed over the tip of Florida and then in much diminished form came over this house.

I sat with my son and granddaughter at an open window and watched all that furious nature go ripping by. Some limbs blew down and we were without power for a day and night. But the principal toll was on our nerves. That saddness and anger I described above was right there waiting. The only cure: A good night's sleep.

Originally published in *Chronicles*

Charleen On My Mind

CHARLEEN SWANSEA IS A PRESENCE, one of those human dynamos who's continually pounding our freewheeling kilowatts. With luck we've all had at least one such person in our lives, someone who energizes and shoves us in the right direction…or, at least, in some direction.

Charleen would not advocate a single right direction or answer for anyone, in any situation. And a "right direction" is not the message of her book, *Mindworks: How to Become a More Creative and Critical Thinker*. Published by SCETV, this self-help workbook lays out easy-to-follow guidelines for attacking stagnation and complacency. Her advice: Just think young. See each situation with the open-minded wonder of a six-year-old and then add to this fresh outlook the mature judgment gleaned from a lifetime of experience.

Sounds simple? Well it is if you're Charleen. If there's a complaint about *Mindworks*, it's just that the book, though invigorating, is not a substitution for meeting with Charleen in person. This problem is partially solved by an accompanying video and totally solved by the seminars she gives around the country. She's in demand, a much-honored educator and scholar, probably better known outside of South Carolina than in—ironic since the Charleston area has been her home for almost ten years.

We weren't total strangers. I shook hands with her once at a party she gave, and I'd seen her in Ross McElwee's award-winning documentaries, *Charleen* and *Sherman's March*.

Her home is on the back side of the Isle of Palms, one of two dozen similar beach structures, but Charleen's is garnished with red geraniums. My knock is timid. She's on the phone, but I'm to make myself at home. The furniture is modern, hard, black and shiny. On the walls, prints and paintings, on the floor, children's toys. An electric organ faces the glass end of the living room, a view of uninterrupted tidal marsh.

I sit in one of the deeply cushioned sofas and study the object on the coffee table: a human brain, convoluted gray matter floating in formaldehyde inside a glass cube. More like a clever piece of modern art than....

Charleen is back—an outwardly generous and friendly woman. She wears a black pants suit of some shiny material, sashed at the waist. There's coffee to make. She smiles. Blond hair that's almost a trademark. As an icebreaker I was going to ask if she preferred being called "The Jane Fonda of the Mind" or "That Blond Broad." But I don't need an icebreaker and the interview starts . . . almost starts, that is. I sit, but she stands and gets ready to deliver a monologue off the cuff. I have definite questions to ask. I can tell it will be give and take. She settles into the sofa across from me and stays there, more or less, except when she's standing or sitting beside me, answering the phone, or making another pot of coffee. And she answers the questions. Sometimes more, sometimes less. The one-hour interview takes three.

What are your origins? Who are your people?

Welsh origins. My people are preachers. All earned a living running their mouths. They came over from Swansea, Wales, with Welsh miners. Never went underground. They just preached against sin and self-indulgence, at which they were masters. Pennsylvania and Georgetown, South Carolina, are where they landed. So, in a way, I think I've come home.

She goes on to laugh about all the towns named Swansea she has visited, and about how she's never found a namesake relative. The subject of relatives, though, seems to bring up some bad memories. Not long ago, she lost both her husband and her island home in a tragic fire. Then Hugo left her temporarily homeless again. There's a deep grief here that I scramble to avoid: No questions about husband or hurricane, I note. But she's already smiling again and telling about the rebuilding of her house.

What is "creativity," how do you teach it?

You don't approach creativity. You live it. It's an attitude. Everyone is born creative. Culture and handicaps of life wring it out of us. I collect toys in an effort to retain what God gave us in the beginning—the ability to be creative enough to enjoy life and find our way in it. (She motions around the room.) I keep them around me all the time—magnets, koosh balls, rubber snakes. They help me retain the attitude of wonder I was born with. It gives me the ability to survive a life of pain and crisis.

How, as a young girl, were you able to meet Albert Einstein?

I had a voice scholarship to Princeton given by the Baptist Church. After a week they decided my talents as a singer weren't good and put me in conducting class. I was a little girl. I was told to pretend I had a quarter tucked in my buttocks. It worked at first, but when I lost control of the music and the teacher asked me what was wrong, someone in the orchestra said, "She dropped the quarter." An old man in the back of the auditorium laughed. I ran out crying and he followed to apologize. That was Einstein. At lunch he would play Bach on the church organ. He went for walks with me. He played childlike games.

Did that meeting change your life?

Yes. It gave me a vivid model of how to keep life in balance. Recreation, play is an important part of the creative mind set.

The Red Clay Reader*? You're probably the only person to run a literary review at a profit. How'd you do it?*

Creativity and hard work. You can't do without either. A capacity for detail. Without it nothing runs well or long.

Do you believe in inherited memory—Jung's common racial memory? How about Wilbur Cash's Mind of the South*? Do you think Southerners can escape their Celtic heritage?*

I believe in creative consciousness for all men and women, and my experience is if we know how to tap into this consciousness by sitting quietly or thinking creatively, we can transcend our private egos, family concerns. *The Mind of the South* is a part of me. I have to go through it. You can't deny it.

[Charleen's young assistant, Kay Durst, arrives. They're doing an experiment with soybeans, all the healing properties of which have yet to be discovered. Kay leaves and Charleen, using both hands with fingers spread apart, almost succeeds in explaining brain chemistry to me.]

Where is the id located? [I point to the cube-contained brain on the coffee table.]

I don't know where it the id is, [She picks up the cube, examines a dangling bit of flesh where two lobes come together, and mutters] but I'm pretty sure that's the seat of the libido. [Louder, she clarifies] Fool! Jackass! [She means me.]

Freud thought creativity was rooted in neurosis. Why don't you?

Freud was a sexist pig. [The remainder of her response is unprintable.]

What do you see when you look at a black dot? [This is a question from *Mindworks*.]

A black hole. What are black holes, really? I'm reading three books about them now. [Her physics and mathematical explanations go right through me—don't even bother to pass over my head. The black dot reminded me of a total eclipse of the sun, and I don't even understand how eclipses work. Still, she's happy with the question and forgives me for the one about the id.]

You mention in Mindworks *that you can double your client's profits if you can come up with a campaign to market pantyhose to men. How do you do it?*

[As ridiculous as this sounds it is an actual question facing the hosiery business, and to print the answer would be a form of industrial espionage.]

One of my sons had creativity enhancement in place of standard college English. Do you think that's an even swap?

English, as we were taught, was taught poorly. I'm committed to the concept of "liberal arts," but the coursework has to connect. Information should integrate our lives. *Mindworks* attempts to supplement, not substitute for, education. It's a way of putting things together.

Some people tend to associate happiness with complacency. Why don't you?

Because I know better.

A good way to end. We go to lunch at the golf course club house and discuss the usual: life, death, sex, money, children, jobs. We agree on most matters but hard differences remain. She eats everything on her plate and claims that life is just beginning. I pick out the scallops, stir the pasta with my fork, and say that life is just about over. Outside, the sunlight brightens my prospects, but I'd still like to escape without a commitment to a better more creative life. No. I can't leave without a ten-day supply of soybeans. They'll make me feel better. Maybe braver.

Like a fairy tale Jack, I wave goodbye to Charleen, confident, at least, of a ten-day supply of bean stalks. After that, there are giants to kill.

Charleen was a trip. And best of all she was right. Life was just beginning.

Originally published in *charleston* magazine

Second Season

September is the kindest month
Breeding locals from the tired sands.

THAT'S TRUE. T.S. ELIOT wouldn't have said it if it wasn't. He almost said it, anyway, and it's still true. Have you ever noticed the beach after Labor Day, how the surf fishermen sprout like mushrooms after a healing shower? Have you noticed how the pace slows? Joggers give ground to walkers and walkers begin to stroll.

It's the summer tourists. They've gone home to jobs and all the other worries of the world. And lest we forget, the children are gone, too—whistled away by the pied piper school boards.

Now, don't get me wrong. I like tourists. I've been one myself. The same with children. I've been one of those, as well. It's just that September is ours, and October, too—golden months nestled between the staggering heat of August and the Northeaster chill of November. These are the months of tempered ease and contemplation. The beach belongs to us—the wise and ancient ones. Yes, that's anyone wise enough to live in South Carolina and ancient enough to have experienced at least twenty-four birthdays.

"Elbow room!" cried Daniel Boone.

Now the weather. If you exclude an occasional hurricane, our weather really is "better." We've got less rainfall now than during the sweltering summer months and warmer temperatures than the spring ones. And this warm, dry air brings prettier sunsets—with a fine orange glow that lingers an eternity. That means T-shirts and shorts into the evening and the feel of night air browsing your skin. The ocean is glowing, too. You're not imagining that. In September the water begins to clear and a phosphorous extravaganza is taking place.

Nature runs in cycles. While you drowse away the morning listening to the radio and struggling with that last bit of tan, animals are bracing for winter. Birds are busy getting fat and sassy and preening away the summer's wear. The fish are biting. These are surely the best months for Spot-tail Bass. But don't forget the trout and, of course, the flounder. And the Spanish mackerel are hitting those big mirror lures—hitting them like furious freight trains. And pound-and-a-half- to two-pound pompano are biting on those sand fleas right under your toes.

Morning glories are blooming. And so are sea lavender and brown-eyed susans, and the marsh, itself, is taking on a golden hue. I suspect it's been brushed by those sunsets.

You can still get the last of the home-grown tomatoes. The shrimp are big, plentiful and fresh, particularly fresh if you caught them yourself, and the same for the crabs, which are fat and active. Boiled crabs and ripe, red tomatoes and then nothing between you and the hammock.

I grow old, I grow old
I will wear my trousers rolled.

Have you noticed how the fashions shift? There's less neon green and day-glow orange being worn and more tans and gentle violets.

And I can let my stomach hang over the front of my bathing suit. You can do that in the golden months, and you can waddle out waist deep in that grand ocean and slap at the salty surface with your palms. Then you can look up at that absolute blue sky and thank the powers that be for another perfect fall at the beach—this blessed second season.

Apologies to those of you who are on a summer vacation—you can always slip back to the Lowcountry for a long October weekend. I put some of this together by asking my neighbors what they liked about the fall, but that last paragraph is all mine.

Originally published in *South Carolina Wildlife* magazine